I.S. PETTEICE

SELL YOUR SOUL

I0092415

All Rights Reserved
Copyright © 2023 by I.S. Petteice

No part of this book may be reproduced or transmitted,
downloaded, distributed, reverse engineered, or stored in or
introduced into any information storage and retrieval system, in
any form or by any means, including photocoptying and recording,
whether electronic or mechanical, now known or hereinafter
invented without permission in writing from the publisher.

ISBN: 979-8-88945-457-1
eISBN: 979-8-88945-458-8

Brilliant Books Literary
137 Forest Park Lane Thomasville
North Carolina 27360 USA

Printed in the United States of America

CONTENTS

FOREWARD

We are put on this earth for one reason and that is to serve our Maker. About three-fourths of our population does not want to hear those words. And quite a few do not even believe there is a God. The people that do not believe in God, or do not want to believe there is a God, do not want anyone else to believe it either. They do not want to hear the word "God,"—ever – any place, any time, in their presence. It is not to be used in schools, and certainly by the Democrats. It is a term to be washed out of the English language. The Democrats and Socialists want to make you ashamed to admit you are a Christian so that you will not talk about it. This makes it easier to make the citizens of this country bow down to socialism. Welcome to the United Socialist States of America.

I

Democratic Socialist Party

When you get complacent and stop paying attention to what is going on around you, you soon find out that you have no freedom.

You should never listen to a politician with contentment or take them at their word. When Congress lies to us, it is just when a politician uses a slogan. Never repeat it.

For instance, did anyone know what "hope and change" really meant? And now everyone chants "move forward" and no one really knows what "move forward" means, but you are finding out that it means moving forward to a socialist government, moving forward to more people on unemployment, moving forward to even more people on food stamps, moving forward to even more deficit; and all the things this government cannot afford. You are now learning what "move forward" really means for your future, because if you had taken the time and energy to find out before the election, maybe you would not have voted for Barack Obama. Somehow more of what you had that was not working seemed better than voting for a scary Mormon, was that it?

For all of you who voted for the Democratic Socialist party, what happens in the future will be on your head. It is your fault. It will be your responsibility now. You will be held accountable, not only by your peers but by God Himself. The next time we have a terrorist attack, we will blame you, because we do not have a leader. We have a Marxist apologist. When you graduate from college, plan to keep going to school if you can find financing, because you will not be able to get a job. There are no decent jobs available for college graduates and ObamaCare, a crime against democracy, will see to it that small businesses continue to close and there will be even fewer jobs available. And who funded ObamaCare? AARP. All of you that joined AARP so that you could get discounts at hotels and restaurants – discounts that you never used or got but the idea was there, so you joined AARP. Soon the government will be bankrupt so you will not be able to get welfare or food stamps either. But then, I do not know how you will continue to pay for your education, because the government will be bankrupt and unless you have wealthy parents or a rich Uncle who has not given all their money to Uncle Sam, you will not be able to continue paying for your education.

It is your fault the energy prices are skyrocketing because Obama's Environmental Protection Agency has shut down the energy-producing states.

When Iran becomes nuclear, we will hold you accountable because you think it is better to have a Muslim in the White House who bows down to the Arabians and apologizes for America instead of a scary Mormon.

Bowing to Russia, making deals behind our back, and telling Medvedev to explain to Putin how he will have more flexibility in his second term, should have been a warning to you, so we will also hold you accountable for this pass.

The fact that a budget has not been passed since the President has been in office should have shown you how weak he is. He has never attempted to work with the Democrats or Republicans in Congress. If he does make a suggestion and Congress does not like it, instead of attempting to negotiate, he leaves and runs back to his office to write an Executive Order. This one is also on your head. Have you read any of his Executive Orders? He is like a petulant child throwing a temper tantrum.

Do any of you ever watch a legitimate newscast? I am not talking about MSNBC, Bill Maher, or even Jon Stewart. I am talking about the local evening news, or better yet a national news broadcast station like Fox that gave you honest and truthful broadcasts. You will find most of the foreign countries distrust America. Each time Obama visits a country, he gives the same speech about how they are our closest ally and each country has heard that same speech before because he just gave it to the last country he visited. Foreign countries do not like or respect him. But that is your responsibility because you decided to put him in office – again.

We began this 2013 election term with Obama putting the U.S. $6 Trillion in debt. If he does end his 4-year term, we will be 10 trillion Dollars or more in debt. That is more than Bush and every other President we ever had together. Now who is Obama going to blame this time? This burden is upon you. Who is going to pay the debt? I am glad there is no one else to blame. What a burden to put on your children and grandchildren. Obama's idea of getting us out of debt is to put us into more debt. He is addicted to spending. Will someone please cut up his credit cards?

Our military has been treated so badly by our government. It is a crime that nearly half of them did not even get to vote. No one seems to mind that this is in violation of their Constitutional rights. The fact that our young men no longer want to join the military because they are no longer proud of their country – well, that is on your head too. It is despicable how our military men and women have been treated by this administration. And for you complainers, there is nothing wrong with showing a picture ID to vote. Voting is a privilege and why would you not want to show a picture ID so that someone else cannot vote in your place? It is a requirement in the State of Nevada and frankly, I am glad no one else can vote under my name. It is the ones that are committing voter fraud that do not want to show an identification and they are the ones that should be investigated.

Are you having trouble getting a loan to buy a home? That will continue under this administration. It is not going to get any better. People selling their homes must retrofit their homes at great expense because of ObamaCare. The housing market is so low that they have to sell at a great loss. But worse yet, the banks just are not lending any money to buyers. They are holding so many foreclosures that they do not even have them listed on the market. If they listed them, the market would fall even further. It is very difficult to buy or sell a home.

More and more people are becoming dependent on food stamps. A few months ago it was 46 million. Now it is nearly 50 million. But that is part of socialism and you voted for socialism. The government wants you to become dependent on them. In November 2012, the U.S. Department of Agriculture reported that a record 47,102,780 individuals received food stamps.

According to the U.S. Census Bureau data, that figure exceeds the combined populations of Alaska, Arkansas, Connecticut, Delaware, the District of Columbia, Hawaii, Idaho, Iowa, Kansas, Maine, Mississippi, Montana, Nebraska, Nevada, New Hampshire, New Mexico, North Dakota, Oklahoma, Oregon, Rhode Island, South Dakota, Utah, Vermont, West Virginia, and Wyoming.

Since January 2009, the number of individuals on food stamps has increased rapidly from 31.9 million to the current record high million. By comparison, in 1969 just 2.8 million Americans received food stamps.

What about employment? Are you out of a job? Are you even looking for a job, or did you give up looking? When I was growing up, going on unemployment was a last resort, sort of like going on welfare. First, you started pounding the pavement looking for a job or jobs. If you had to take two part-time jobs, so be it. But you did not sign up for unemployment except as a last resort. It was called pride. What happened? Did socialism take us that far? Did we forget what it was like to hold up our heads and take care of ourselves instead of letting the government take care of us? It seems like Congress just keeps extending your benefits. Now people will not take a job because they can make more money on unemployment than they can make working.

Obama has a dream of a World Government with him at the head. That could happen with the downfall of Greece and the breakdown of some of the other European countries. Are you ready for another Hitler, because that is what he will become?

Are you ready for the UN to govern the United States instead of our having a Constitution? Obama said our Constitution is getting in the way of his doing what he needs to do.

And you so readily agree that China can control the world trade and trample all over us. You voted for that one also.

Did you even think about the loss of our freedoms that we knew in the past? Did you really think your life would go on as before? Wake up! Your nightmare is only beginning.

Just think; a dictatorship instead of a democracy that follows the Constitution. It is all yours.

If you are fortunate, you will get to work more hours per week, but you will get less take-home pay and higher living costs. It is already happening. You are bringing home less money now. I say if you are fortunate, but chances are your employer will not be able to afford to give you more hours, and in some instances, your employer will be putting employees on part-time so he does not have to pay benefits. As soon as the election was over, some small businesses started closing. Some closed because of ObamaCare and some closed because the unions stepped in and thought they would take over. Unions and Socialism cannot work together. But Obama owes the unions because they spent about a billion dollars to get him elected. As soon as the tax hikes went into effect, most of you saw a noticeable difference in your paycheck and it was not to the good. You are bringing home considerably less money. These taxes were supposed to only affect the wealthy, but that just did not happen.

For those young people, please do not even consider social security as a retirement plan. Also, do not consider an IRA plan either. Already there is a bill requiring all businesses to automatically enroll their employees in IRA plans in which part of every employee's paycheck would be automatically deducted and deposited into this account. If this passes, the government will be just one step away from being able to confiscate all these retirement accounts. This will be the same as the government spending social security funds. Start your personal retirement account now. You are the only one you can depend on, not the government.

Your next car will look like a toy because it will be government-mandated. It will either be electric, or fuel efficient, and the only vehicle allowed on the road.

When the recession gets worse, and I believe it will, I will blame you, the Godless Democrat.

When the border at Mexico blows up again and there are more deaths, and there will be, it will still be your responsibility. Obama continues to refuse to close the borders. There are those with more grace than I who give the Mexicans a pass for voting for Obama. I do not. Most Mexicans I believe are Catholic or Christian and they did not vote for their religion, and this will fall back on them. Perhaps they feared their loved ones would be deported. I do not know, but I do know many of them have been in the United States for more than 20 or 30 years and have had plenty of time to become citizens of this country and have never bothered to apply for citizenship. They want all of the benefits, but they do not want to become a citizen. If they do not want to become a citizen, they should be deported. Many of them are here just to work only and support their families. They are not interested in becoming assimilated and becoming Americans. Some have never even learned the language. Obama is attempting to grant them immunity and it was his promise in order to get their votes. But Congress, hopefully, will never allow this to happen. They must follow the laws that are already in place. The fact that Obama released Mexicans from prison was a mistake and this too will fall back on you because you voted for him. These Mexicans are repeat offenders and should never have been released, or at the very least should have been deported to the very bowels and jungles of Mexico.

ObamaCare needs to be repealed. No one read it before it was signed. It has many provisions that have nothing to do with health care. It is really bad for senior citizens. It will reduce the number of doctors in this country. It will bankrupt our Medicare system and the government. The Democrats still have not read the Bill yet refuse to reform it. I agree it should not be reformed. We cannot afford socialized medicine. People complain that the poor need medical care. The poor have always had medical care and they still get medical care in this city. The costs of ObamaCare are continuing to increase and that is on your head.

The Benghazi situation is not over and there will be many more. That is your responsibility. It needs more investigation. Obama and Hillary told too many lies on this one. His policies and decisions encouraged the attack on the Consulate. Impeachment proceedings should be started by Congress.

We continue to have government corruption and lies and you continue to give Obama pass after pass. Can he do nothing wrong? You have an obligation, a duty, a responsibility as a voter to see that the buck stops here and truth and honesty start someplace. The government will demand more tolerance of extreme and fanatical Islamists. Terrorist attacks will be called "workplace incidents." But you voted for it. If you stand for tolerance and passiveness, you will find yourself living in fear of your neighbors. So far, we still have freedom of speech, but only if we are being politically correct. That is called Socialism. When will you start fighting back? You sure did not show up at the ballot box.

Has it ever occurred to you that everyone has rights, does not like it should leave. If they [Anglos] do not like Mexicans, they ought to go back to Europe." [interviewed on radio station KYIV, Los Angeles, June 17, 1998.]

A Professor at the University wrote the following poem:

> Haunani-Kay Trask, (Professor of Hawaiian Studies at the University of Hawaii at Manoa, and author of the following poem) except white people? If a Mexican or a black man uses hate speech towards a white man, it just might not be politically correct, but nothing will be done or said about it because anyone saying anything about it would be called a racist. For instance, Mario Obledo (former California secretary of health and welfare and co-founder of Mexican American Legal Defense and Educational Fund:

"We're going to take over all the political institutions of California. California is going to be a Hispanic state and anyone who doesn't like it should leave. If they [Anglos] don't like Mexicans, they ought to go back to Europe." [interviewed on radio station KYIV, Los Angeles, June 17, 1998.]

A Professor at the University wrote the following poem: Haunani-Kay Trask (Professor of Hawaiian Studies at the University of Hawaii at Manoa, and author of the following poem)

Racist White Woman
I could kick Your face,
puncture Both eyes.
You deserve his kind Of violence.
No more vicious Tongues, obscene Lies.
Just a Knife Slitting your tight Little Heart.
For all my people
Under your feet
For all those years
Lived smug and wealthy Off our land
Parasite
Arrogant
In your painted mouth, thick With money And piety

Grace Watkins (black 18-year-old New Yorker on two policemen killed in a shootout at the Stapleton Houses project where she lives): "I think a lot of people out here weren't worried about [the killings] because they thought they were white cops. But when they heard the cops were black, their attitude changed totally. And they started expressing concern for the police officers' families." [Douglas Montero, "Surprising Sympathy Dawns in Projects," New York Post, March 12, 2003.]

Charles Barron (New York City Councilman, on the subject of reparations for slavery) — "I want to go up to the closest white person and say: 'You can't understand this, it's a black thing' and then slap him, just for my mental health."[Deroy Murdock, "Dems Need to Houseclean" National Review Online, January 6, 2003.] Sharpe James (mayor of Newark, New Jersey referring to his light-skinned black opponent in the 2002 Democratic primary) "the faggot white boy." [Deroy Murdock, "Dems Need to Houseclean" National Review Online, January 6, 2003.]

Spike Lee (film director) — "When talking about the history of this great country, one can never forget that America was built upon the genocide of Native Americans and enslavement of African people. To say otherwise is criminal." [Lee Gives 'The Patriot' a Thumbs-Down, Los Angeles Times, July 7, 2000, p. F2.] Ice Cube (black rap musician) — "Ice Cube wishes to acknowledge white America's continued commitment to the silence and oppression of black men.... White America needs to thank black people for still talkin' to them 'cause you know what happens when we stop." [pamphlet included in his 1992 album The Predator.]

John Street (black mayor of Philadelphia) — "Let me tell you: The brothers and sisters are running this city. Oh yes. The brothers and sisters are running this city. Running it! Don't let anybody fool you; we are in charge of the City of Brotherly Love. We are in charge! We are in charge! [Cynthia Burton, "Street Talk Hits a Nerve on Race," Philadelphia Inquirer, April 17, 2002, p. A1.]

Miles Davis (black jazz musician) "If somebody told me I had only one hour to live, I'd spend it choking a white man. I'd do it nice and slow." [Miles Davis Can't Shake Boyhood Racial Abuse, Jet March 25, 1985.]

Khalid Abdul Muhammed (former assistant to Louis Farrakhan—current leader of the New Black Panther Party)– "Hollywood is owned by these so-called Jews. Look at the movies they make about us, Black people killing Black people. Let's make some revolutionary movies where we kill white people in the movie. Kill 'em so hard you have to cover up your popcorn from the blood spraying out of the screen." [Speech at San Francisco State University, May 21, 1997.]

Art Torres (former chairman, California Democratic Party)– "Remember, [Proposition] 187 [the measure to cut public benefits to illegal aliens] is the last gasp of white America." [The Social Contact, Summer 1998, p. 290.][1]

There are many more quotes at this website. The point is that if the white man said these things about a Hispanic or a Black man, they would decry racism or worse yet, hate speech and file charges against you. Yet we are supposed to just say they are not being politically correct. There is indeed racism in this country. But the fact is it is not coming from the white people. Untold trillions have been spent on welfare, food stamps, rent supplements, Section 8 housing, Pell grants, student loans, legal services, Medicaid, Earned Income Tax Credits, and poverty programs designed to bring the African-American community into the mainstream. Churches, foundations, civic groups, schools, and individuals all over America have donated their time and money to support soup kitchens, adult education, daycare, retirement, and nursing homes for blacks. You hear the grievances, but you never hear the gratitude.

Martin Luther King came a long way in healing the rift between the blacks and the whites. But I think the whites accepted it more than the blacks. The blacks just never seemed to be able to let go. They like playing that blame game and still blame the whites for everything. They keep talking about how the whites made them slaves but slavery has not been in existence in 150 years and none of the blacks of today have been affected by slavery. They all have had the same educational advantages as the whites, but they do not show up for class. What is their anger toward the whites? I see blacks in big business. I see blacks making big bucks. Do the angry blacks think they should not have to work to get where they want to be? Do they think the whites have not worked hard to get where they are? Whites do not hate blacks. It is my opinion that whites have accepted blacks as equals the same as all other races.

Then Obama became president and he has done more to ruin relations between blacks and whites than any other president. He is constantly calling out racism when and where there is none. He has set back the gains made by Martin Luther King over the years.

---

[1]   http ://rense.com/general50/ pcc.htm

Everybody blames education, but it is not the education. It is parenting. The parents have to make that child go to school and when that child comes home from school, the parents have to make that child do the homework. You cannot blame the teachers if your child fails the class. Your child has to read the books, complete the assignments, and attend class and you, the parents, are the ones that have to see that he accomplishes that end. If you do not do your part, you have no one to blame but yourself when your son becomes a gang member and does not graduate from high school.

II

Socialism

On November 6, 2012, Americans voted for Socialism instead of Capitalism. Like it or not, we then became the United Socialist States of America. In the early days of America, Socialism was attempted but was abolished because it produced more takers than givers. We have that now. Every may jack wants something for nothing. Everybody wants an Obamaphone. And they got one in exchange for their vote for Obama.

For you older people that do not know what an Obamaphone is, you will remember the days when we did not have telephones at all and some of you still do not have a cell phone. Now Obama is giving them away free to "financially unstable" persons. Even this program he blames on the Bush Administration when he says that Bush introduced a project that gave subsidies to those that could not afford a phone so that everyone could at least call 911. Remember when we used to reach out to our neighbors and knew our neighbors by their first names? There may have been only one neighbor on the block that had a telephone and that was probably a party line. Today, no one can look you in the eye and say hello. They do not know how to communicate with you in person. Everyone has a phone of some kind in their hand, or in their ear. They do not see what is going on immediately around them. The idea is that there are several deaths every year and everyone should have proper communication. You are going to die whether you have a cell phone in your hand, or not. Chances are, if God calls your number, you will not get to dial 911. But the free Obamaphone even offers some texting, and rollover minutes, and has different plans so the "unstable" can pick out which plan is best for them.

Everybody wants on the food stamp program. Some are on drugs and do not have a decent place to call home. They get their check, get their food stamps, sell the food stamps to make more money, and buy drugs. They do not have to worry about having a meal because they work the system. They get their meals free by going to the Salvation Army or a flop house on Main Street. But they do collect the food stamps. And they hang out on the corner near McDonalds or Taco Bell and pander for your quarters so they can save up for their next fix.

We enable the people on unemployment. We enable the people on the food stamp program. I am not saying there are not some people that need to be on the program. But I am saying there are many that are abusing the system. All you have to do is work in a grocery store and see the people pay for their groceries in food stamps and go out and load them into a brand new truck and drive off and you know they are abusing the system.

Years ago we had a proverb that said "Give a man a fish and he will eat for a day. Teach a man to fish and he will eat for a lifetime." Now we have a Liberal Proverb. It goes something like this: Give a man a welfare check, a free cell phone with unlimited free minutes, free internet, cash for his clunker, food stamps, section 8 housing, free contraceptives, Medicaid, ninety-nine weeks of unemployment, free medicine, and he will vote Democrat the rest of his life...even after he's dead.

People on the system are watching the news, some for the first time, because they fear if Congress does not reach an agreement on this fiscal cliff issue that they will have to go out and look for jobs as not reaching an agreement affects whether or not their unemployment checks will be extended. Personally, I was hoping an agreement would not be reached so these leeches would have to get off their bottoms and go out and find a job, because they have not looked for work in over two years. I know that for a fact on several people. They have not even looked for a employment.

There is a true story of one woman in Ohio that said she found one way to get around the system when she was at a Kroger store in Goshen, Ohio and a person was in front of her in the grocery check-out line who was a white female, approximate age 35-43, fake nails, big braided hair do, clean clothes, carrying a purse and a plastic drinking cup. This person put her purchase on the check-out surface – one grape. Yes, that is correct one grape. The cashier asked if that was all, she replied yes. The cashier then weighed the grape and told the women the cost was $.02 (two cents), the women then pulled out her EBT card (credit card for food stamps) and swiped it through the credit card machine, requesting $24.00 in cash back. The cashier asked if she wanted the grape and the woman replied no and the GRAPE was put in the garbage can. The register recorded the sale as $.02, cash back $24.00, credit $.02, total $24.00 cash back. The cashier then asked if two fives would be okay because she was out of tens, the woman agreed and took the $24.00 folded it up and put it in her pocket and left the store. As the next person in line, I asked the cashier "as a tax payer what in the hell just happened here?" She said she was on the clock and could not comment. She then asked if she had actually seen this person purchase and discard a grape, then get cash back on her EBT card. The cashier responded that it happens all day every day in their store. She also said that if the person buying the grape has it ring up over $.02 they get mad and make her reweigh it. Her next comment was to ask the cashier if she planned to vote in November and she said she could hardly wait for 11/6/12 to get there.

Some states, such as Ohio, say that a person is eligible for food stamps on income alone and do not take into account other resources such as savings accounts, stocks or belongings such as cars. You can have $20,000 in a savings account, but if you do not have a job, apparently you can get food stamps.[2]

Everybody wants on welfare. Back in 1964 this writer worked in the Family Court System in Illinois. A family with 11 children came before my Judge. They were receiving $1,100 a month from welfare. That was a lot of money in 1964. The father could not go out and find a job making that kind of money to support that many children.

We currently have eleven states where more people are currently on welfare than people that are employed. Seven of those eleven states voted for Obama. The majority of Americans have no intentions of making a better life for themselves and their families and are content living on the tax payers' dime.

Today many women keep having babies because the more babies they have, the more money they make from welfare. It does not matter to them whether they can properly take care of the children, or whether the children have fathers. It is the money coming in every month that they worry about. They are out there for anything they can get free. A lot of people on welfare give up necessities like insurance because they have to give up luxuries like having their nails done or having their hair done, or they cannot have all the up-to-date gadgets. These people are criminals and should be prosecuted. Instead, they are teaching their children how to defraud the government.

Remember when we were growing up and we were taught that you paid your bills before you put food on the table. Remember how mom and dad scrimped and scraped to pay their bills and how when we were getting started we sometimes had to take more than one job to keep us going, even if it was temporary.

I grew up in the WWII era and it was extraordinarily poor times. We walked up and down the railroad track to collect the coal that fell off the coal cars from the trains that went by. Besides the coal, we chopped wood to burn to get us through the cold winters and for cooking. We picked wild strawberries alongside the railroad track so mom could make strawberry jam for the year. We picked wild raspberries and blackberries, which mom canned for pies, cobblers, and

---

[2]   http://timesgazette.com/main.asp?SectionID=1&SubSectionID=1&ArticleID=162992

berry dumplings throughout the year. We dug sassafras root so mom and dad could have tea during the cold winter months.

I climbed more than one cherry and apple tree to pick enough for canning. We always had a garden to be tended and canned at the end of the summer so we could have fresh vegetables during summer and canned vegetables during the winter months. We raised chickens, ducks and rabbits, along with pigs and cows for meat and we had a cow for our dairy products. Churned butter is a lot different than what you purchase in the grocery store. And we had a separator that we put the milk through each night to separate the cream from the milk so we could make the butter. We made fresh homemade cottage cheese. No one does that anymore.

Welfare? We would not think of it. Mother nature and God provided for us. We lived a couple blocks from the school and every day after lunch after the kids went back to school, mom would walk along the road and pick up the lunch sacks the kids threw away, because quite often the kids threw away store-bought cookies that they had not eaten, and that night after we had supper, mom would spread out before us this treasure trove of treats.

There was a government assistance program in those days, but you had to be really destitute and disabled to even think about applying for it. My family never did. My father was crippled from polio as a child, but he worked harder than any other man. If we were able-bodied at all, we made it on our own. Now our entire welfare system is out of control. People that are able-bodied go on it just because they do not want to work.

Everybody wants to get on the unemployment line. I take that back. There is not a line anymore. You just make a telephone call. You do not even have to go out and look for a job to be qualified. You just call in and say you are still unemployed and they extend your benefits. That makes it easier for people to defraud the system. I know people that have been on unemployment for 2 years and do not even look for a job. I have told them of jobs that are available and they tell me they get more money on unemployment than they can get working at McDonalds. So they would rather sit at home watching their big screen television sets all day that they got with their EBT card, or playing computer games all day, or hanging out with their friends that are also not working. In all my working life, I never one time went on unemployment.

The number of Americans designated as "not in the labor force" in February was 89,304,000, a record high, up from 89,008,000 in January, according to the Department of Labor. This means that the number of Americans not in the labor force increased 296,000 between January and February. The Bureau of Labor Statistics (BLS) labels people who are unemployed and no longer looking for work as "not in the labor force," including people who have retired on schedule, taken early retirement, or simply given up looking for work.[3]

Then there are the ones that are ripping off Medicaid. Some need help in the home because they are very sick and need nursing care or meals brought in because they are unable to cook or clean or provide for themselves. Then there are those that ruin it for the needy because they rip off the system and make millions of dollars off the system every year by overcharging Medicaid for services that were never rendered to the sick and needy. Since the government started doing audits, billions of dollars in fraud have been discovered. The problem is it usually can only be discovered by agencies and not individuals. A person enters the hospital and their caretaker continues collecting money for caring for them because they do not want to start the process all over again. The states do not monitor the program.

There is a problem with all of that taking and the government giving all those freebees. The government is broke and is now looking for ways to make money so they can continue to give you freebees.

> "When the people find that they can vote themselves money, that will herald the end of the republic."
> —Benjamin Franklin.

Socialism, social and economic doctrine that calls for public rather than private ownership or control of property and natural resources. According to the socialist view, individuals do not live or work in isolation but live in cooperation with one another.

---

[3]   http://conservativebyte.com/2013/03/record-89304000-americans-not-in-labor-force/#ixzz2N9xgObwY

Furthermore, everything that people produce is in some sense a social product, and everyone who contributes to the production of a good is entitled to a share in it. Society, therefore, should own or at least control property for the benefit of all its members. It is characterized by production for use rather than profit, by equality of individual wealth, by the absence of competitive economic activity, and, usually, by government determination of investment, prices, and production levels. This conviction puts socialism in opposition to capitalism. Another term for Socialism is Marxism.

In a socialistic society, the government controls all means of production. Obama wants everyone dependent on the government. He already has 47 million people on food stamps. He has done nothing about creating jobs. He has instead put more people on unemployment and continues their benefits so they will give up looking for employment. Unemployment will continue during his second term.

Although Barack Obama never refers to socialism or Marxism, he does constantly refer to everyone having a fair share, which is a Marxist term. There are many people in this country that unashamedly claim to be socialist. Most democrats are socialists. They prefer to say Liberal However, if you read the Declaration of Independence, you will find that our forefathers came to this country and founded this nation and our Constitution in order to get away from the socialists of Great Britain.

If you read the Federalist Papers and other writings from our Founding Fathers, they knew we would eventually move toward socialism, and they wrote our Constitution the best they possibly could in order to prevent that.

Karl Marx said that capitalism will eventually fail and that communism is the solution and end game. He said you can wait for that to happen, or you can accelerate the process by overwhelming the system and destroying capitalism. If you are a business owner, you are aware that Obama has imposed several thousand new regulations on businesses in just the last three months. That does not include the massive amount of regulations imposed over the past four years.

Once the system is overwhelmed and you destroy capitalism, you implement communism. Americans are too ignorant to understand what communism will do for them so they need to be forced down that path by any means necessary, whether it be by lies, deceit, creation of class and race warfare issues and use of catastrophes. This is why when Obama talks about anything, it is always dramatic and the world will end if we do not do it right away.

According to Karl Marx, if the progress is not fast enough, you need to kill people to help the greater good achieve enlightenment. That is why in Russia they killed – for the greater good. Of 60 million of their own people course the greater good is so that the top 3% in government leadership can have all of the power and wealth and remove all means for the masses to ever be able to topple them, including taking all rights, taking all weapons, and eliminating religion.

Obama's favorite college professors are Marxists. Obama's favorite books were written by Marxists. Obama's parents and grandparents were Marxists. Obama's friends are Marxists. Obama's administration is full of Marxists. They no longer call the term "Marxists." They now use the term "Progressives."

Americans do not believe this could happen in this country. They go to work every day and go about their business every day and come home and prepare their evening meal, spend time with their family, talk on the telephone, maybe watch a program on television, go to bed and the next day do the same thing all over again. Many do not know who their Senators and Representatives are for their state. Some do not know who their Governor is. Some do not know who their Mayor is. Many have never watched the evening news or read a newspaper and this is what Obama counts on – all the ignorant people in the world. That, and all of the entitlement society.[4]

Now, a little more than 200 years later this country has voted to turn this country into a socialist country. The next level up from socialism is communism. Barack Obama has already told Comrad Medvedev that he would be more flexible during this second term.

To try to put it more simply: The philosophy of capitalism is Capital (or the "means of production") is owned, operated, and traded for the purpose of generating profits for private owners or sharehold-

---

4   http://www.impeachobamacampaign.com/obamas-latest-attempt-to-overwhelm-the-system/

ers. Emphasis on individual profit rather than on workers or society as a whole. The philosophy of Socialism is from each according to his ability, to each according to his contribution. Emphasis on profit being distributed among the society or work force in addition to receiving a wage.

The ideas of Capitalism are Laissez-faire means to "let it be"; opposed to government intervention in economics because capitalists believe it introduces inefficiencies. Free market produces the best economic outcome for society. Government should not pick winners and losers. The ideas of Socialism are all people should be given an equal opportunity to succeed. Workers should have most say in their factory's management. The free market suffers from problems like tragedy of the commons. Government regulation is necessary.

The Key Elements of Capitalism are the accumulation of capital drives economic activity–the need to continuously produce profits and reinvest this profit into the economy. "Production for profit": useful goods and services are a byproduct of pursuing profit. The Key Elements of Socialism are Economic activity and production especially are adjusted to meet human needs and economic demands. "Production for use": useful goods and services are produced specifically for their usefulness.

The ownership structure of Capitalism is the means of production are privately-owned and operated for a private profit. This drives incentives for producers to engage in economic activity. The ownership structure of Socialism is the means of production are socially-owned with the surplus value produced accruing to either all of society (in Public-ownership models) or to all the employee-members of the enterprise (in Cooperative-ownership models).

The Economic Coordination of Capitalism is it relies principally on markets to determine investment, production and distribution decisions. Markets may be free-markets, regulated-markets, or may be combined with a degree of state-directed economic planning or planning within private companies. The Economic Coordination of Socialism is Planned-Socialism relies principally on planning to determine investment and production decisions. Planning may be centralized or decentralized. Market-socialism relies on markets for allocating capital to different socially-owned enterprises.

The political movements of Capitalism are Classical liberalism, Social liberalism, Libertarianism, Neo-liberalism, Modern Social-Democracy. The political movements of Socialism are Democratic Socialism, Communism, Libertarian Socialism, Anarchism, Syndicalism.

The key proponents of Capitalism are Adam Smith, David Ricardo, Milton Friedman, Fredrich Hayek, Ayn Rand. The key proponents of Socialism are Robert Owen, Pierre Leroux, Karl Marx, Fredrick Engels, John Stuart Mill, Albert Einstein, George Bernard Shaw, Leo Tolstoy, Emma Goldman.

The way of change of Capitalism are fast change within the system. In theory, the relationship between buyer and seller (the market) is what fuels what is produced. Government can change rules of conduct/business practices through regulation or ease of regulations. The way of change of Socialism are Workers in a Socialist-state are the agent of change rather than any market or desire on the part of consumers. Change by the workers can be swift or slow, depending on change in ideology or even whim.[5]

Most Socialist are Democrats. Socialists do not care about God or His Word. Remember the Democratic National Convention when they stood and shouted "No, we don't want God."

People losing their homes? This is a good thing to the government. People become more dependent on the government. Old people about to lose their home in this economy? That is even better. Just take out a reverse mortgage. If you are lucky, you might break even or even make a couple bucks. But you won't make what the house was worth a few years ago. And if something happens to you, the house will not be worth enough for your family to come in and repurchase it at your death and guess who gets the house – Uncle Sam. The only good thing is that you don't have to make any house payments, but you do have to pay the taxes and upkeep on the house. And any money you take out of the house, Uncle Sam tells you how you can and cannot spend it. ObamaCare has a provision whereby

---

5   http://www.diffen.com/difference/Capitalism_vs_Socialism

you have to retrofit your homes or mobile homes in the event you decide to sell them. They must meet certain government criteria, a large expense to the owner.

Obama certainly will not do anything about closing the borders and every illegal will be crossing the border to get free welfare, food stamps, housing, education, and more. Who do you think is going to pay for this? Anyone that has a job, and the unions will have to pay. Watch what happens when Obama says you should take a cut in pay to "distribute the wealth." That will bring it closer to home for you. What happens when the rich move somewhere else? Why would you want to live where you have to support over half of the population? This is happening in Europe already; particularly in France.

We have been on the road to slithering socialism since the early 1900's and the Rockefellers. FDR was a socialist. George Soros is probably the worst one I have read about and Obama is the one that will take us down the road to total socialism. That is why he fought so hard for reelection. That is what his term "move forward" means. It is his sole agenda.

We need limited government, not more government. We need to cut spending, not more spending. Tax increases are not the answers to making our small businesses grow. We need a Congress that will stop surrendering and that will stand up and stop making deals and do what is right for this country. We put them in office and then they walk out on what they were put in there to do.

Obama thinks France has the ideal government, but the citizens of France are starting to rabbit. The President of France has raised the tax rate to 85%. A French Actor recently moved to Belgium because of the tax raise. Besides being an actor, he is an entrepreneur and created and invested in restaurants, wine bars, and vineyards. As he says, "80 people are working thanks to me, in companies that were created for them and are managed by them." He invested money and created jobs. But when property is plundered, entrepreneurship is discouraged.

Indeed, why take so many risks, work so long, and invest so much for the few peanuts that France's welfare government deigns to leave in the entrepreneur's bank account? In addition to being social-ists, all of them are civil servants or members of government-subsidized organizations. Subsidies and appointments have nothing in common with earning a living and being hired. That is another reason why the welfare government "elite" cannot understand businessmen. He said in addition, the President is trying to push through a 75% income tax, plus a higher "wealth" tax, higher capital gains taxes, higher inheritance taxes, and a tax on selling your business, among other taxes. "European countries are just a few years ahead of the U.S. in terms of becoming more socialist, with an insatiable demand for more of your income to pay for ever-growing government programs." I think the same thing will eventually happen in this country. Right now the rich are saying they are happy to pay a little extra. But eventually they will get sick of it and I will not blame them. I do not think they should be paying it now. They earned it and the people getting the freebees and not trying to get a job are not entitled.

In 1938, Austria was in a deep depression and voted to allow them to be annexed to Germany and have Hitler to be their Ruler. They had "heard" great things about Germany such as no unemployment, no crime, and a high standard of living. They had not heard anything about the persecution of the Jews. They were just told that a vote for Hitler would mean a better life and that the farmers would get their farms back and there would again be food on the table.

Hitler decided women should have equal rights and put both the men and women to work. They lost religious education for the children and all religion was taken out of schools and replaced with praises to Hitler and Deutchland.

Food was rationed and could only be purchased using food stamps. There was a law that if you worked you could get a ration card and get food stamps. If you were unemployed, you did not get a card and stamps and you starved to death if you did not know how to live off the land. It was compulsory for all youngsters, male and female to give one year of service to a labor camp and at night they returned to barracks for military training.

When a mother went into the work force, the government had child care centers with people trained in child psychology where it took care of all children free of charge for all children 4 weeks of age and up.

Just like ObamaCare, Hitler had socialized medicine. Doctors were salaried by the government. If you needed surgery, you had to wait up to a year so the best doctors immigrated to other countries. That is how it is in Canada and England now.

Then Hitler said people should register their guns, so the people did. Then Hitler said people should turn in their guns. Well, the people had just registered them, so their names were known, so they could not hide the guns.

America better wake up. This is all happening to America right now. Our government wants to set up free child care for our mothers with government trained child psychologists caring for your children. Our government has taken religion out of our schools. Our government has sanctioned our school children singing praises to Obama in school. It will be very soon when our food will be rationed. But way more than 47 million people are already on food stamps. Our government wants a national gun registry and the purpose for that is to get the name and address and number of guns of every gun owner in America so the government can confiscate America's guns.

From what I have researched, progressive socialism in America began in the early 1900's. At that time America was a strong Christian nation and that was the one thing that had to be overcome. The progressives had to work within the churches and make the Christians question the Bible. You have seen some of the stories on television where the scientists come up with ways to dispute the Bible and there are movies out completely distorting Bible stories. Hollywood came out with a movie saying Jesus was not born of a virgin and that he married and did not die on the cross, but moved to France. And many progressives believed it and they began planting seeds of doubt all over America.

Then all of a sudden you started hearing about women clergy, then gay clergy, and divorce rates for the Christian world was as common as the rest of the world. Pretty soon everyone is living together before marriage, and then no one is getting married anymore. More people are in bars on Saturday night than are in church on Sunday morning.

The progressives also knew they had to destroy the family unit. Remember when mom did not work and when dad came home from work at night everyone gathered around the table for dinner at night and you actually had a meal together and talked about your day? Sometimes dad owned his own business and sometimes he worked for someone else. But those were honest, hard-working days. But the same tactics used to weaken the Christian influences were used to weaken the family unit. The ideas of divorce became easier than working out problems and turning to the Bible. Kids learned to blame all their problems on their parents. The Socialists infiltrated the schools and changed what was being taught. They are not taught anything about family values.

Planned Parenthood teaches your daughters how to get an abortion and work around parental notification laws.

Remember when you used to watch television and there was always a stay at home mom and a strong father figure and kids that respected their parents? When you watch television today, the families are dysfunctional and never represent a traditional family. It is always a single mother or father trying to cope. They say that is because it represents what we have today.

Then you have the homosexual issue that completely destroys the traditional family values. A homosexual relationship can never be the same as the relationship between a man and woman and the procreation of their offspring. Homosexuals have to use unnatural means to try to accomplish the same thing, and it just does not allow for the same wholesome bonding and upbringing of children.

The last thing that has to be accomplished is the Progressive Socialist has to make the people dependent upon the government for their very existence and livelihood. The government must become their master and they become the slave.

Under Obama, a record-number of Americans have gone on welfare programs, disability and food stamps. One in four children are on food stamps. Oh, wait! That is another thing Obama does not like the name of. It is now called Supplemental Nutrition Assistance Program. Between Medicaid, food stamps, unemployment and other government assistance programs, people cannot afford to go out and get a job at minimum wage. They would lose money and benefits.[6]

Are we headed for Socialism or Marxism in this Country? Yes. Our first steps to socialism were when we nationalized major sectors of our economy. That is what our bailouts were. Then you keep hearing about redistribution of wealth. That is what ObamaCare is; a redistribution of wealth. Next is to discredit their opposition – the ones that will rally against them. Our government, through Homeland Security, issued orders to law enforcement agencies throughout the country, future threats to America were right wing Christian groups, pro-life groups, Second Amendment groups, and returning veterans, but did include Islamic terrorists. Then we have censorship. Hate crime legislation has been passed so that pastors will not get in the pulpit to preach against the homosexuality or same sex marriage, to censor them. Gun ownership has to be controlled in a Marxist movement. If the President signs the small arms treaty, the UN will decide how you and I, as Americans, will buy and sell weapons.

THE FINAL THING IS HOW TO DEVELOP A CONSTABULARY FORCE. PRIOR TO THE ELECTION THE PRESIDENT SAID IF ELECTED HE WOULD HAVE SUCH A FORCE – IN THE HEALTH CARE LEGISLATION IT STATES THAT IN TIME OF CRISIS THE PRESIDENT SHALL HAVE A FORCE AS LARGE AND AS WELL-EQUIPPED AS THE MILITARY. IT TALKS ABOUT A COMMISSION OF OFFICERS – A CONSTABULARY FORCE THAT WORKS FOR THE PRESIDENT THAT WILL CONTROL THE POPULATION IN AMERICA. THIS IS LIKE RUSSIA TODAY; LIKE CHINA UNDER MAO TZU TUNG. LIKE HITLER WITH THE BROWN SHIRTS BEFORE HE BECAME AFRAID OF THEM.

---

6   http://politicaloutcast.com/2013/01/american-socialism-working-1-in-4-kids-on-food-stamps/#ixzz2Hn8SG47f

I am tired of hearing that it is only fair that the wealthy pay for the rest of us. That is Marxism. The rich pay 70% of taking care of their neighbors. The Prince of this world seems to be Satan. Karl Marx said "Religion must be destroyed." Now do you understand what is going on in our White House?

Are you socialist enough to attend the funeral of Venezuelan President Hugo Chavez? Reverend Jesse Jackson, Congressman Gregory Meeks (D-NY) and former Congressman William Delahunt (D-MA) are and did attend the funeral.[7]

NA05KWpe "We pray God today that you will heal the breach between the U.S. and Venezuela," Jackson said.

---

[7]   http://conservativebyte.com/2013/03/u-s-congressmen-join-sean-penn-at-chavez's-funeral/#ixzz2

III

Welfare

Any man who thinks he can be happy and prosperous by letting the Government take care of him, better take a closer look at the American Indian." — Henry Ford

The Senate Budget Committee calculates that "the amount of money spent on welfare programs equals, when converted to cash payments, about '$168 per day for every household in poverty.'" This is higher than the $137 median income per day. Here is the math: $168 per day x 365 days = $61, 320.

I know if someone gave me $61,320 per year and I did not have to pay Federal, state, or Social Security taxes on any of it, I could live quite comfortably on that amount. Probably most families in America could if they chose a modest lifestyle. Not only is it tax free, but you do not have to work for any of it. We keep hearing about the rich paying their fair share, but the poor get paid to do nothing but sit at home and play computer games all day. They do not have to go to work and pay their fair share. It is given to them.

Government employees almost always vote democrat. Their jobs are assured as long as they do. As long as payments are made to the poor, the poor also vote for Santa. Santa is whoever is in office.

This is a country where if you are self-sufficient, you are a threat to the government.[8] So what does the government do? It complains about the senior citizens and spends our social security money that we worked for all our life. It dumps our social security money into the general fund so they can spend it faster than we can replace it. Then they come up with ObamaCare and tell us when we reach age 75 we need to think of an alternative lifestyle. Remember when Dr. Jack Kevorkian was the rage and we called him Doctor Death because he assisted really sick people in their suicides. Now ObamaCare calls it mandatory that we meet with a death panel and the government will gladly help us end our days. It is more money in the government coffers. Why prolong any illness and keep us alive any longer than necessary. It is the Grim Reaper Government Style at your service "we have to read it to find out what is in it," thank you Barack Hussein Obama. Never mind the senior citizens, we are going to make sure you barely subsist. But it is not really a death panel. It is a sneaky test that you will not even know about. They call it a Mortality Test. You will not even know you are taking the test. The doctor will ask questions like what is your age, sex, weight, height? Do you have diabetes? Do you have chronic lung disease? Did you smoke during this week? Do you have congestive heart disease? Do you have difficulty walking several blocks due to your health? Your answers to these questions will determine the type of treatment you receive on the illnesses you have after the ages you attain after you are 70. And for you, the babies, we will make sure you never make it at all. Mom, you can get that abortion, if you want to. The government did not stop to think about the people on Welfare that cannot afford to buy insurance. And in 2014 when the IRS begins to fine everybody $95 that does not have insurance because they are on unemployment or on Welfare – oh, did we forget about that angle. You do not have to worry that you will someday be old. And you do not have to worry that Congress and the President are not on this ObamaCare plan. Should we not always be mistrustful of what Congress hands out to us when it is not first rate enough for them?

---

[8]   http://politicaloutcast.com/2012/12/could-your-family-live-on-61320-per-year-tax-free/#ixzz2EV6h3h2g

20% of the government budget goes on the military, defense, and international activities. According to all parties, it is untouchable.

21% of the budget goes to Medicare, Medicaid and the Childrens Health Insurance Program (CHIP). An additional 13 percent goes to safety-net programs like SSI, food stamps, school meals, housing and childcare assistance, etc. "These also are untouchable," according to the redistributionist class of both parties.

20% is paid for Social Security, which provides retirement benefits to 35.6 million workers and other benefits to another 19.8 million spouses and children of retired workers, spouses and children of deceased workers, disabled workers and their eligible dependents. Social Security is considered an entitlement program, but it should not be since it is supposedly funded by money confiscated from workers — who had no say in the matter — to fund their retirement. The program was long ago looted by the elites and is the biggest Ponzi scheme in history. "Social Security is sacrosanct and untouchable," leadership of both parties lie to you as they confiscate the funds faster than they pour in.

Representative Tom Price (R-Ga.) says Obama's plan to increase taxes on the rich will generate only enough revenue to fund the Federal government for eight days. What he does not tell you is that income taxes do not fund the government. They are simply a wealth redistribution/information gathering tool used by the government.

Government debt is a world-class delusion. It is a tool used to justify theft and redistribution. And it has worked to perfection,

Pitting the have-nots against the haves, while the one percent (government workers and elected class) make out like the bandits they are. Meanwhile, many become even more embittered over the idea that someone may have a greater pile of worthless green paper strips than they do.[9]

During the Reagan administration, only 19% of the U.S. households did not pay any income taxes. During the Clinton administration, that figure jumped to 25%. During the Bush administration, 30% of the U. S. households did not pay any income taxes. Since

---

9   http://personalliberty.com/2012/12/03/the-fiscal-cliff-is-a-mirage-but-a-real-cliff-is-ahead/

Obama has been in office, this figure has increased to 47%. Obama wants America to become dependent on the Government.

Eleven states have more people on welfare than employed. Guess who those states voted for in the November election. Those states are Hawaii, California, New Mexico, Mississippi, Alabama, South Carolina, Illinois, Kentucky, Ohio, New York, and Maine. I watched a video of a young woman in California being interviewed about the welfare system. She said that California welfare system is the best, they pay the most on EBT. You get money for free daycare but most people just have their friends take care of their kids and they split the money. You get cash. Dominos Pizza accepts EBT, McDonalds accepts EBT. Subway accepts EBT. Most fast food places accept EBT. It is easy to get cash on the system. She said we get $221. She said "why would we want to go to work"?

There is something wrong with a government that takes money from those that work hard for it and gives it to those that do not want to work for it.

IV

Our Society And Liberals

I believe our society started changing in the 1960's. I am not sure of exactly why or how.

Perhaps my parents' generation saw things changing and held on too tightly and people like me rebelled. My sister was okay, but I was the rebel in my family. It was an environment of being seen and not heard and nothing was up for discussion and after a while, I blew and made everybody's life totally miserable. But life changed for a lot of other people also. Some decided that life was going to be better for them than it was for their parents and they were going to raise their children differently. They were more lenient in their child rearing methods. Along came Dr. Spock who believed in time outs instead of spanking a child because we didn't want to damage their little personalities. Children had been receiving spankings forever and all of a sudden parents believed one man because he said he was a psychiatrist, whose own child, by the way, committed suicide. I think that was when we became the tolerant society. Children became less disciplined and felt less loved, and got away with more. Now we are asking ourselves why our children have no consciences and why it does not bother them to kill their classmates and themselves. Parenting today seems to have been replaced with Ritalin and a lot of video games.

Many parents stopped going to church altogether. Some still believed in God, but some, as time went by, grew further and further away from God. They never bother watching a church program on television on Sunday morning, or bother sending their children to Sunday School. Some believe the Bible even to be a myth or just a book of stories and even watch programs on television that promote this theory that compounds this belief. Instead of raising their children to go to church, or to believe in God, or telling their children about God, their children also watch the same programs on television, and never learn to believe there is a real God.

So instead of learning about God's Love and the Ten Commandments, the next generation has learned that good is a little on the square side and tolerance is better.

They learned that when you watch television or use the internet, dirty movies and pornography or swinging is more fun than just being straight. That if it feels good, it must be okay. But you cannot put a nativity set in a public park during Christmas. What they do not learn until it is too late is that prisons are overflowing. In 2004, one in every 138 residents is locked up. That costs the U.S. taxpayer $49 Billion a year. That is a staggering number and amount. That was 28 years ago. It has to be much higher at this time. Then we found out there are no such things as criminals. They are now called "sick people." And more money is spent on trying to rehabilitate them than is spent on the victims. Most of the "sick people" are never rehabilitated and are habitual and cannot live in society and San Francisco has one of the highest rates of recidivisms in the state. Some 78.3% return to prison within three years of release according to a report from the California Department of Corrections and Rehabilitation.

You decided to run God out of your schools and what were the consequences of that decision? Children started carrying guns to school and now you have to have metal detectors at school. You have to have hall monitors. You have more drugs being sold on the school grounds. You have a lack of respect between the children, and between the children and the teachers. There are rampant teen pregnancies, increased foul language, committing crimes or felonies, and listening to ungodly music. In addition, every parent should have a responsibility to read the books from which the children are being taught. You might be amazed at some of the new "very liberal" ideas that are being taught to your youngsters. You decide that marriage is outdated and it is okay to just live together, or just go out and have sex. It is the in-thing now to go to a bar and walk up to someone and ask them if they want to have sex. You have the attitude that if it feels good it is okay. Have you no morals at all or is everyone amoral? This is where a religious background would have been helpful to you. Believe it or not, everything in the Bible has been proven to be true. The only thing that has not been found are the walls of Jericho. The Bible has some wonderful true stories in it and is worthwhile reading. It does teach about marriage being between a man and a woman. And if you are going to bring a child into the world, for its sake, I hope you will think about getting married first. Marriage is to be a sacred bond. Husband, love your wife with all your heart and do not undress every woman you pass on the street. The Bible does say it is a sin when you lust after other women. The same goes for the Wife.

We now have nearly every state promoting gambling to make money. There are only two states that do not have some form of gambling: Alaska and Hawaii. Yet there are only 9 states that are capable of depending on a gambling income and not imposing an income tax on the people of that state. They are: Alaska, Washington, Nevada, Wyoming, South Dakota, Texas, Tennessee, Florida, and New Hampshire. I have lived in Nevada since 1971.

There is nothing worse than to see a senior citizen going to the casino on payday, cashing their social security check, and sitting at the poker machine until it is gone. Nevada, having a warmer climate than many states, also has a larger number of homeless. I am guessing, but I would believe we have more bankruptcies than any other state because of gambling. People look at gambling as a way to get rich. They do not look at the hotels and casinos and see how they got so big and luxurious. They just think that they too, will get rich. Nevada also has a large number of Gamblers Anonymous meetings at all hours of the day and night, every day of the week, where hundreds of people attend.

You took God out of Easter and made the symbol a basket of colorful eggs and candy for the kids to play and eat. Do your children have any idea what Easter means? Have you ever told them the real story of the crucifixion, or do you even know yourself?

You took God out of Christmas and made the symbol a holiday tree. We used to call it a Christmas tree and used to have a Nativity Scene under it because it was the celebration of the birth of Jesus Christ. That was the purpose of this holiday; the birth of Jesus Christ. Then somebody got the idea they wanted the holiday, but they did not want to celebrate the birth of Christ and they did not want the rest of us to celebrate His birth either. And the liberals and the socialists said okay, we do not want to offend anyone, so we will all celebrate this holiday and everyone has to say Seasons Greetings or Happy Holiday, but no one can say Merry Christmas anymore, and no one can display a Nativity Scene. Well, you celebrate your way, but at my house we celebrate the birth of Jesus Christ and if you knock on my door I will say Merry Christmas because I am still a Christian. When I am able to put up my Christmas tree, underneath I proudly display the nativity scene that I made 60 some years ago and since it is my home, I do not care if this offends anyone.

Churches are at war with themselves and with each other. The Catholic churches are fighting amongst themselves and with the Pope. The Pope tells them to do one thing and they do not follow his orders. The protestant churches are having the same problems. It seems as though our government is being most of the problem. We have many liberal priests and preachers these days. The priests and pastors used to be very strict and taught their parishes from the Bible. Now they do not seem to agree so much with the Bible on many subjects such as gay rights and abortion issues.

While some priests and parsons were telling their congregations to vote the Bible, others were not, and freely speak out on their views on these subjects. You can go to any church, but it is rare that you will find a preacher that will preach the Bible like it says. He is afraid to tell the Congregation what the Bible says for fear that he will offend someone. Yet many of the Congregation are there because they want to hear the truth of God's Word.

The Preachers need to wake up and stop being liberal because they too are accountable to God. How about the fact that we just trash God? God is suppressed in school and the work place. Then you have the hate speech laws that are in effect to guarantee that the preachers will not preach certain sermons.

Unfortunately, we cannot legislate morality. Our laws are all moral laws, representing a system of morality. Whenever you weaken the religious foundation, you weaken the morals of our society.

You now see many nations at war amongst themselves. Libya, Syria, Egypt, Afghanistan, only to name a few. We are nearing another revolutionary war in this country.

The Media in this country is probably the worst in the world. When I was growing up I remember thinking if you ever had a big problem you should go to the media. But the days of Watergate is over. I never saw such liberal socialism as MSNBC and most of the media because they cannot and will not and other stations are not much better. I would not consider watching any station other than Fox. I just get angry. There is no such thing as good reporting anymore.

And now, because of our Godless country and Godless ways, we have an elected Godless President that is a socialist/marxist that wants to take from those that earned what they have, and give it to those that want it and did nothing to earn it. When political correctness and tolerance becomes the way of our society, we have lost the cherished values of our founding principles.

We need to put aside our apathy and unconcern for what is going on around us and in our government and start fighting for our liberties. America is now a divided nation with half of the country embracing socialism. We need to stop the growth of anti-American policies and restore the Constitution and adherence to the principles that made America great.

If the patriotic citizens of America do not band together, we will lose our freedom.

If you look up the word Liberal, you might find some of the following definitions: (1) favorable to progress or reform, as in political or religious affairs. (2) noting or pertaining to a political party advocating measures of progressive political reform. (3) of, pertaining to, based on, or advocating liberalism. (4) favorable to or in accord with concepts of maximum individual freedom possible, especially as guaranteed by law and secured by governmental protection of civil liberties. (5) favoring or permitting freedom of action, especially with respect to matters of personal belief or expression: a liberal policy toward dissident artists and writers.

The most instrumental party for a liberal is the Democratic party as it is favorable to progressive or reform. It favors the maximum individual freedom possible, especially with respect to matters of personal belief or expression: a liberal policy toward dissident artists and writers. It is free from prejudice or bigotry; tolerant: and has a liberal attitude toward foreigners. Democrats are normally liberal and more progressive. They usually are pro-choice, anti-military, higher taxes for the rich which would support social programs that help lower income and senior Americans. Democrats also normally believe in bigger government.

As you know, conservatives favor tradition and generally suspect things that fall outside traditional views of "normal." You could say that a liberal, or progressive, view is one that is open to re-defining "normal" as we become more worldly and aware of other cultures.

Liberals favor government-funded programs that address inequalities that they view as having derived from historical discrimination. Liberals believe that prejudice and stereotyping in society can hamper the opportunities for some citizens.

Liberals favor censorship of Christianity and are often anti-Christian, or otherwise disagree with moral or social principles held by many American Christians.

Liberals favor increased government spending, power, and control. Many liberals favor a welfare state where people receive endless entitlements without working.

An increasing number of liberals have sided with the homosexual agenda, including supporting homosexual "marriage".

A liberal generally will support the following agendas:

- Spending money on government programs Government's ability to solve economic problems.
- The belief that terrorism is not a huge threat, and that the main reason for Muslim extremists' hostility towards America is because of bad foreign policy.
- Taxpayer-funded and/or legalized abortion.
- Censorship of teacher-led prayer in classrooms and school/state-sponsored religious events.
- Support for gun control.
- Affirmative action.
- Opposition to government regulation or restriction of obscenity, pornography and violence in video games as a First Amendment right.
- Government-funded medical care, such as ObamaCare.
- Taxpayer-funded and government-controlled public education.
- Insisting that men and women be placed in the same jobs in the military.
- Legalized same-sex marriage and homosexual adoption.
- Tax and spend.
- Support for economic sector regulations.
- Support and spreading of political correctness.
- Support of non-syndicalist labor unions.
- Encouraging promiscuity through sexual education (the teaching of safe sex) rather than teaching abstinence from premarital sex.
- A "living Constitution" that is reinterpreted as liberals prefer, rather than how it is thought to have been intended.
- Government programs to rehabilitate criminals.
- Abolition of the death penalty.
- Environmentalism.
- Globalism.
- Support for the constitutionally mandated separation of church and state.

- Opposition to full private property rights.
- Reinstating the Fairness Doctrine.
- In 2005, it was reported by CBS News that liberals were the most likely supporters of the theory of evolution.
- Opposition to domestic wire-tapping as authorized in the Patriot Act.
- Opposition of Operation Iraqi Freedom, a major part of the War on Terrorism.
- Withholds support to the War on Terrorism and the War in Iraq.
- Tolerance of different ideas and lifestyles.
- Do not support a laissez-faire capitalist economy and support regulation of business.

Liberals currently use two clauses to try and expand their power: the Commerce Clause and the General Welfare Clause. The general welfare clause mentions "promoting the general welfare". This to a liberal means taxing the rich at increased rates and redistributing that money. The commerce clause, on the other hand, says that Congress has the power to regulate trade with foreign nations, between the states and with the Indian tribes. Since the days of FDR this clause has been interpreted very loosely and has resulted in the Federal government expanding its power. The latest example is The Affordable Care Act (ACA), better known as ObamaCare. In the ACA, the liberals justify the individual mandate by saying it regulates commerce between the states.[10]

Liberals like to change the names, or terms, or things. It is a ploy to get you used to thinking their way. For instance, we no longer have illegal aliens. We now have undocumented workers. You no longer receive Social Security checks. You now receive Federal Benefit Payments. If you get that into your head long enough, perhaps you will forget that you worked all your life and earned that money yourself, along with the contribution of your employer and start believing that the government is giving you a check each month out of the

---

[10] http://personalliberty.com/2012/12/03/the-fiscal-cliff-is-a-mirage-but-a-real-cliff-is-ahead/

goodness of their heart. Also, you are not supposed to call terrorists by that name anymore either. I think it is because they are all of the same descent, but it would not be tolerant if you called them terrorists. I guess we are not supposed to talk about them at all.

When Obama became President, the Liberals felt free to "come out of the closet." Where they pretty much kept their opinions mainstream before 2008, they now decided this was their time to shine. For Christians, it was like someone let the devil and all of his imps out of Hell.

Now all of a sudden the liberals were telling everyone we did not need God in this Country (see clips of the Democratic Convention). The liberals are telling us that everyone should be pro-choice and all the Democrats voted pro-choice. The liberals are telling everyone that same sex marriage is okay. Our President will not enforce the Defense of Marriage Act (DOMA). The Liberals are pushing gay rights in everybody's face. The liberals are attempting to take away our first and Second Amendment rights. Our Father in Heaven is going to be really busy on Judgment Day.

I do not know about you, but I am tired of liberals telling me I have to be politically correct about everything. I have had enough of that crap. And I am tired of the Christians having their Civil and Religious rights taken away from them and replaced with Islam. And I am tired of hearing that it is okay to be racial and slam everyone or be just plain nasty and offensive if you are a comedian as if that gives you a special license and a pass.

If you would fit the entire world into a village consisting of 100 people maintaining the proportions of all people living on earth, that village would consist of 57 Asians, 21 Europeans, 14 Americans (North, Central and South), and 8 Africans. There would be 52 women and 48 men. There would be 30 Caucasians and 70 non-Caucasians. There would be 30 Christians and 70 non-Christians. There would be 89 Heterosexuals and 17 homosexuals. 6 people would possess 59% of the wealth and they would all come from the USA. 80 would live in poverty. 70 would be illiterate. 50 would suffer from hunger and malnutrition. 1 would be dying. 1 would be born. 1 would own a computer. 1 (yes only one) would have a university degree.

Illinois lawmakers are attempting to pass a bill to make same-sex marriages legal. Chicago Mayor Rahm Emmanuel has endorsed the measure. In the business community, leaders of Google, Morningstar, Private Bancorp Inc. and Groupon have also publicly endorsed the legalization of same-sex marriage. Another big money man to support the bill is Fred Eychaner, a Chicago media mogul who donated $14 million to Democrats in last year's elections. Laura Ricketts, co-owner of the Chicago Cubs, and a publicly professed lesbian, is also supporting the bill. David Smith, Executive Director of Illinois Family Institute pointed out that only about 250 of the thousands of priests, ministers and rabbis have endorsed same-sex marriage, indicating that the vast majority of them do not favor it. He commented about the bill, saying: "I think it's a little bit of an overreach. In fact, I have challenged the sponsor of the bill. If he is so confident that the people of Illinois want same-sex marriage, then why does he not put it on the ballot and let the people decide? The general public in Illinois rejects the idea of redefining God's institution of marriage. Marriage is one man, one woman — Always has been. Always will be. It's almost as silly as proposing that we change the definition of triangles to circular. There is no such thing as round triangles. There is no such thing as same-sex marriage."

V

Executive Fiat

When Ronald Reagan came to the Presidency, he declared that Government was not the solution to our problems. Obama never did try to hide his ambitions. In an address to Congress in 2009, Obama declared his intentions to transform America in three areas: health care, education, and energy. Health care is one-sixth of our economy. Education is the future. And energy is the lifeblood of any advanced country. Control pricing and production and you have controlled the industrial economy. This is by far the largest spending bill in history–$830 Trillion Dollars–lavishing large amounts of tax dollars on favored companies and industries in a bare display of industrial policy.

What Obama could not pass through Congress; he enacted by Executive Fiat. He could not pass Cap and Trade, but his EPA is killing coal. In his second term, natural gas will follow coal. Obama's Environmental Protection Agency regulates fracking into noncompetiveness. He put thousands of coal miners out of work during his first term. An Obama second term means that the movement toward European-style social democracy continues, in part by legislation, in part by executive decree.

Obama loves Executive Orders. He hates negotiating, so when someone says no to him, he turns and leaves, goes to his office, and writes an Executive Order.

Obama has poured literally millions of our American dollars into energy programs that have gone bankrupt.

Abound Solar, for instance. Abound is a manufacturer of cadmium telluride thin-film photovoltaic modules that was based in Colorado. It was incorporated in 2007 and received a $400 Million loan from our government. The company filed for bankruptcy protection in 2012.

Amonix, a solar manufacturing plant headquartered in Seal Beach, California, opened an office in North Las Vegas, Nevada in 2010. What better place to have solar panels than in the desert. But Amonix soon declared bankruptcy. They too had received a $21.6 Million loan from our government. Sources said ""I don't think they had a lot of training." "There were a lot of quality issues. A lot of stuff was coming back because it had some functionality issues." But the Amonix plant was highly touted by political leaders. Nevada Senator, Harry Reid, U.S. Representative, Shelley Berkley, D-Nev., and Nevada Governor, Brian Sandoval, were among the political leaders who lauded the company when it announced it would start making solar panels. Reid in particular has pushed for solar energy research and development in Nevada, drawing parallels between the value of Nevada sunshine and Saudi Arabian oil. The North Las Vegas plant was a joint venture with Singapore's Flextronics Industrial. Amonix founder and Chairman, Vahan Garboushian, had estimated capital investment of $15 million in the plant, including equipment, construction and tenant improvements. In July 2010, President Barack Obama talked up the Amonix plant during a Nevada visit to support Reid's re-election, saying tax credits for the plant provided by Federal economic stimulus efforts had already made an "extraordinary impact."

Not only has Babcock & Brown, an Australian Securities and Investments Commission, fallen apart and filed bankruptcy, but they were indebted to our Federal government to the tune of $178 Million.

Now we have Beacon Power, another investment of Obamas. Beacon received $43 Million from our government before they filed bankruptcy.

Ener1, the parent company of an electric car maker that received more than $100 Million from the Obama administration filed for bankruptcy protection in 2012. The CEO explained this was because the demand was fewer than expected for electric cars. Evergreen Solar, who received $5.3 Million from our government, filed bankruptcy in 2011. They were a Massachusetts clean-energy company that listed $485.6 Million in debt.

Mountain Plaza, Inc., a Tennessee company, received a stimulus from the U. S. Government in the amount of $424,000. The stimulus was approved by the EPA and the Tennessee Department of Transportation for the construction of electrical hookups at a truck stop so truckers would not have to burn diesel while resting. But the stimulus was paid after the company had filed bankruptcy.

Raser Technologies, a Utah company, is Senator Orrin Hatch's Solyndra. They received $33 Million from our government in 2009 and filed bankruptcy in 2011.

Solar Trust of America, LLC., who received $2.1 Billion in conditional loan guarantees from our Department of Energy, holds the development rights for 1,000 megawatt Blythe Solar Power Project in the Southern California desert. They filed bankruptcy in 2012.

Solyndra, who received a $535 Million loan from our government in 2011 will be liquidated under the Bankruptcy Court, but it's parent company 360 Degree Solar Holdings, Inc. will exit court protection with so-called net operating loss carry forwards of as much as $975 million, which it may use against future income, according to court papers. Tax breaks may be as much as $341 Million. Solyndra's collapse prompted congressional scrutiny of President Barack Obama, who praised the company during a May 2010 tour of its facilities. It was the first company to receive a loan guarantee under Obama's stimulus program. But everybody knows that will not lead anywhere.

Spectra Watt, backed by Intel and Goldman Sachs Group, a solar cell manufacturer, filed bankruptcy in 2011. Falling module prices and increased Chinese competition have been cited as the primary reasons. Spectra received $500,000 from our government.

There are many others that our government has assisted that are in the process of failing.

Before the election, a couple of Republican Senators and a Michigan Congressman raised concerns about a Chinese company winning an auction to purchase much of bankrupt battery maker A123 System Inc.'s business. Part of the Republicans' concerns stems from a $249-million grant the U.S. Department of Energy made to A123 to increase its manufacturing capacity. Now that capacity will be owned by a Chinese company. U.S. Sens. Chuck Grassley of Iowa and John Thune of South Dakota echoed concerns they had raised earlier, with Thune calling President Barack Obama's energy policy "a win-win for China and a lose-lose for the American taxpayer." "Shortly before the election, this administration told the American people that A123's government-financed technology would stay in the United States," said Grassley. "This assurance turned out to be false. Now, we need to find out why the administration said this, what classified technology will be at risk, and whether the more than $100 million in taxpayer money given to A123 will end up in Wanxiang's pockets."

BrightSource's LPT solar thermal system is currently being deployed at the Ivanpah Solar Electric Generating System (ISEGS) in California's Mojave Desert. Ivanpah, which started construction in October 2010, is the first project that will deliver power to serve the company's signed contracts with PG&E and Southern California Edison. They received $1.6 Billion from our government and are in distress.

Ecotality, another electric car company based in San Francisco, has partnered with China and owes our government $126 Million. First Solar owes our government $3.1 Billion. It is a company making proprietary thin film semiconductor technology. If you click on their financial statement, instead of getting an actual profit and loss statement, you get a lot hyperbole about how they could compete in China and India and Australia and even Thailand and areas that need more electricity generated. This company was in distress in May of 2012.

Fisker Automotive owes our government $529 Million. Fisker said it would use the bulk of the money to fund the design, engineering and assembly of a next-generation plug-in hybrid car. The car will retail at $39,900, after tax credits, according to a Fisker statement. Fisker has ruled out bankruptcy and is looking to Wall Street for financial investors.

Johnson Controls is a global company in distress that owes our government $299 Million.

In a remote desert spot in northern Nevada, there is a geothermal plant run by a politically connected clean energy start-up that has relied heavily on an Obama administration loan guarantee and is now facing financial turmoil. The company is Nevada Geothermal Power, and it is struggling with debt after encountering problems at its only operating plant. The amount of money the federal government has at stake with Nevada Geothermal — a loan guarantee of $79 million plus at least $66 million in grants.

SunPower is another distressed solar company that owes our government $1.2 Billion.

U. S. Geothermal is a distressed company based in Idaho that received $97 Million from our government.

Each one of these companies at one time employed a large number of employees, but at the present time employ none, or the distressed companies have laid off workers. I would call the energy program of this president a failure and give him a grade of an F and disband the Department of Energy.

As for education, I have always believed that big government should have no hand in education and that it should go back to the states. Obama wants to give everyone free education. He believes every black child's problem begins with its education. He is wrong. Every child, white or black, has a problem with parenting, not education. You cannot keep a child in school if he does not have parental control or parents that are not educated or caring enough to keep that child in school. All the free education in the world is not going to matter to a kid if a parent does not make him go to school or better yet, want to go to school. This needs to be dealt with at the local level and not at the Federal level. Get rid of the Federal Government from our School System.

As to Health Care – For Heaven's Sake – what is the matter with Congress? Repeal ObamaCare now!

VI

Second Amendment

"All political power comes from the barrel of a gun. The communist party must command all the guns, that way, no guns can ever be used to command the party." —Mao Tzu Tung, Nov 6, 1938

"Democracy is two wolves and a lamb voting on what to have for lunch. Liberty is a well-armed lamb contesting the vote." —Benjamin Franklin

Gun control is any law, policy, practice, or proposal designed to restrict or limit the possession, production, importation, shipment, sale, and/or use of guns or other firearms by private citizens. Most commonly the guns in question are personal firearms, typically handguns and long guns.[11]

It seems incongruous that those who call for gun control are always the ones who want the guns so they can have the control. As Americans we should keep an eye on those we have entrusted to serve us. They start out to be patriots and turn out to be crimi-

---

[11] http://www.ask.com/wiki/Gun_control?o=3986&qsrc=999

nals. Look at how many Governors from Illinois went to prison. Do a little goggling and find out how many Federal employees never pay income taxes. Do a little more goggling and find out how many Federal employees in high positions hired by Obama have criminal backgrounds. Or just pick up my book "Soundoff." I made a list of them. Most Democrats are anti-gun zealots and either progressive or liberal in their views.

The biggest threat to our Second Amendment rights are President Barack Obama and Attorney General Eric Holder. Adolph Hitler was elected to a democratic Germany and we are now going down the same road.

Mass murderer Adolf Hitler at a dinner talk on April 11, 1942 said:

> "The most foolish mistake we could possibly make would be to allow the subject races to possess arms. History shows that all conquerors who have allowed their subject races to carry arms have prepared their own downfall by so doing. Indeed, I would go so far as to say that the supply of arms to the underdogs is a sine qua non for the overthrow of any sovereignty. So let's not have any native militia or native police. German troops alone will bear the sole responsibility for the maintenance of law and order throughout the occupied Russian territories, and a system of military strong-points must be evolved to cover the entire occupied country."

Germany established gun control in 1938 and from 1939 to 1945, 13 million Jews and others who were unable to defend themselves were rounded up and exterminated.

Josef Stalin, the sole leader of the Soviet Union from 1924 to 1953, said: "If the opposition disarms, well and good. If it refuses to disarm, we shall disarm it ourselves."

In 1929, the Soviet Union established gun control. From 1929 to 1953, about 20 million dissidents, unable to defend themselves, were rounded up and exterminated.

Mao Tzu Tung, communist dictator of China said: "War can only be abolished through war, and in order to get rid of the gun it is necessary to take up the gun."

China established gun control in 1935. From 1948 to 1952, 20 million political dissidents, unable to defend themselves, were rounded up and exterminated.

Idi Amin, president of Uganda from 1971 to 1979, said:"I do not want to be controlled by any superpower. I myself consider myself the most powerful figure in the world, and that is why I do not let any superpower control me."

Uganda established gun control in 1970. From 1971 to 1979, 300,000 Christians, unable to defend themselves, were rounded up and exterminated.

Pol Pot, who created in Cambodia one of the 20th century's most brutal and radical regimes, was responsible for killing one million of his own 'educated,' yet unarmed citizens.

Eric Holder said "What we need to do is change the way in which people think about guns, especially young people, and make it something that's not cool, that it's not acceptable, it's not hip to carry a gun anymore, in the way in which we've changed our attitudes about cigarettes. You know, when I was growing up, people smoked all the time. Both my parents did. But over time, we changed the way that people thought about smoking, so now we have people who cower outside of buildings and kind of smoke in private and don't want to admit it. And that's what I think we need to do with guns[12] Holder-Fight-Guns-Like-Cigarettes.

Criminal politicians like Obama refuse to look at history. Dictators like Adolph Hitler, Fidel Castro, Mao Tzu Tung, Josef Stalin, Idi Amin, Lenin, and Pol Pot have committed murder to the largest degree. Time and time again it has been a corrupt government who is responsible for the mass murder of their own people under the deceptive guise of "gun control," all of which the said dictators implemented. These people promised their citizens protection and freedom upon the forfeiture of their guns.

---

[12]   http://www.breitbart.com/Big-Government/2012/03/18/

While you were not listening, former U. S. Attorney General, Janet Reno, said "Waiting periods are only a step. Registration is only a step. Prohibition of firearms is the goal."

Killing people is a moral problem that we have in our society today. We do not need more gun control. We need more parental control. We need more families that are willing to spend time together, mom and pop spending time with their children. We need mom and pop taking responsibility for what is going on in the lives of their children.

Gun sales are one of the few industries that has benefitted since Obama's Presidency. Last year background checks hit the 1.5 million mark. In the weeks since the election, gun sales have skyrocketed, especially for AK-47s and AR-15s. It is said that sales have been so high for the AK-47 that ammunition is starting to run low for them. Homeland Security is buying up the AR-15s for their department.

Some people say they are buying guns before the Government forbids anymore sales. But sales have increased since the election and many people are saying they are stocking up on guns and ammunition and food and other supplies in preparation and anticipation of America's collapse, some say by the prediction of the Mayans and Nostradamus, or by Obama himself in the next 4 years. Either way, we are in big trouble. America no longer has faith in our Government.

There are many television programs about preppers and dooms day, and no matter who you talk to, you can find 1 in 5 people that are preparing because they believe that America will fail economically under Obama and the country will go into complete calamity. Food and supplies will become scarce causing millions to riot and loot and steal from one another. People say that they intend to protect their families, their homes and supplies from any and all intruders. They also say that they expect government forces to start confiscating firearms and when they come to their homes, it is going to be a battle to the death.

It sounds to me like another revolution by the American people. That is the one thing that Obama fears the most and the biggest reason he wants to take away their guns. And, if we do not have guns, we cannot stop him. Why do you think no foreign country wants to invade the United States? They know behind every door is a gun and every American that owns a gun knows how to use it. America does not intend to give up her guns.

Gun control is illegal and against the Constitution. What some people are not aware of is that the Second Amendment was devised to protect us from the power of the Federal Government. Originally our forefathers did not arm the American people for the purpose of hunting, but rather to protect themselves from those who were doing the hunting, namely the tyrant King George.[13]

It was men like Washington, Jefferson, Madison and Hamilton that supported the Second Amendment.

True preppers are faced with the possibility of having to rise against their own government and that is truly a scary decision to make. Many will just turn their weapons over along with their freedom.

You must remember that our Constitution is the law and it is undisputable. For one man to come along and attempt to circumvent it or change it to suit his own purposes is illegal and treasonous to the office he holds. Our founders understood that the Constitution could protect the people by limiting the power of anyone to work outside of it much better than a pure system of popularity. A system of checks and balances was set up to help limit corruption of government and also the potential for an "immoral majority" developing within the American People.

Just because many Americans love Obama and voted for him, does not mean that he has the power to go against our constitutional rights. It does not matter how many people support gun bans. It is a violation of our constitutional rights.

The framers of the Constitution were very clear. If the government comes to take your guns, they are violating one of your constitutional rights that is covered by the Second Amendment. If they come for your guns then it is your constitutional right to put them six feet under. You have the right to kill any representative of this government who tries to tread on your liberty. I am thinking about self-defense and not talking about inciting a revolution.

---

[13] http://freedomoutpost.com/2013/01/gun-control-dictator-style-tyrants-who-banned-firearms-before-slaughtering-the-people/#ixzz2JPMRJQto

Re-read Jefferson's quote. He talks about a "last resort." I am not trying to start a Revolt; I am talking about self-defense. If the day for Revolution comes, when no peaceful options exist, we may have to talk about that as well. None of us wants to think about that, but please understand that a majority cannot take away your rights as an American citizen. Only you can choose to give up your rights.[14]

The Obama administration is endeavoring to use procedures and methods of gun control that will impose major damage to our Second Amendment before U.S. citizens understand what has happened. He does not want the American people to have guns and he will do everything possible to see that they are taken away from The People. He has his own agenda and will go to any length to pursue it. Obama can appear before the public and tell them that he does not intend to pursue any legislation (in the United States) that will lead to new gun control laws. Yet, while shrouded in secrecy, his then Secretary of State, Hillary Clinton, committed the U.S. to international treaties and foreign gun control laws. Does that mean Obama is telling the truth? What it means is that there will be no publicized gun control debates in the media or votes in Congress. We will wake up one morning and find that the United States has signed a treaty that prohibits firearm and ammunition manufacturers from selling to the public. We will wake up another morning and find that the U.S. has signed a treaty that prohibits any transfer of firearm ownership.

And then, we will wake up yet another morning and find that the U.S. has signed a treaty that requires U.S. citizens to deliver any firearm they own to the local government collection and destruction center or face imprisonment.

How can this be? It is because no one ever watches the news anymore. It is because no one listens to what is going on in the world anymore. It is because we have a Media that does not report half of what is going on in this country. It is because you go to work each day and come home from work and you are tired and just want to play on your computer or watch some silly, inane program on television and forget everything else that is going on in the world. It is

---

[14]   http://freedomoutpost.com/2013/01/if-they-come-for-your-guns-do-you-have-a-responsibility-to-fight/#ixzz2I4YBJOfP

because you elected a Congressman that you thought was going to do the right thing for this country and someone you thought you could trust and they do not do what is right for you!

Well, la de da, duh! Life does not work that way anymore. You are now living in the United Socialist States of America, or have you not noticed. And if you ever want this country back to where it used to be, you better wake up and start paying attention, because every day more and more of your rights are being taken away from you. Congress does not work for you. They are out for what they can get for themselves. You have to watch their every move – everything they do.

On February 11, 2008, Obama admitted in an interview that he supported a handgun ban, and that it was "constitutional." On June 26, he said he agreed with the Court's decision, but added that the right to bear arms is subject to "reasonable regulations." He never "explained" how an absolute ban on handguns is "reasonable," or how he can agree with the ruling, which said it was unreasonable. Obama continued to duck and cover by talking about getting illegal guns off the streets, background checks for children and the mentally ill, and attacking the NRA.

> "That the Constitution shall never be construed to authorize Congress to infringe on the just liberty of the press or the rights of conscience; or to prevent "The People" of the United States who are peaceable citizens from keeping their own arms."
> —Samuel Adams

> "A free people ought ... to be armed."
> —George Washington

> "Laws that forbid the carrying of arms... disarm only those who are neither inclined nor determined to commit crimes... Such laws make things worse for the assaulted and better for the assailants; they serve rather to encourage than to prevent homicides,

for an unarmed man may be attacked with greater confidence than an armed man."

—Thomas Jefferson

"If the representatives of the people betray their constituents, there is then no resource left but in the exertion of that original right of self-defense which is paramount to all positive forms of government, and which against the usurpations of the national rulers, may be exerted with infinitely better prospect of success than against those of the rulers of an individual state."

—Alexander Hamilton, The Federalist No. 28

"We should heed the warning of James Madison, "Father of the Constitution."

"There are more instances of the abridgment of the freedom of the people by gradual and silent encroachments of those in power than by violent and sudden usurpations."[15]

Obama said, "So I believe in the Second Amendment. It does provide for Americans the right to bear arms for their protection, for their safety, for hunting, for a wide range of uses."

The President made the above comment during a joint appearance with President Calderon of Mexico in March of 2011 when he referenced the flow of guns into Mexico from the United States.

It was nice to hear the President of the United States admit that our Constitution had a Second Amendment and that he believed it, taking into consideration the fact that he and Hillary Clinton have long been attempting to including the United States in a worldwide treaty regulating guns with the UN Small Arms Treaty Agreement. Fortunately, so far anyway, our Congress has intervened, and more than 50 Senators signed a letter to Secretary of State Clinton saying that they will not vote for any treaty that restricts civilian arms. The United

---

[15]   http://www.americanthinker.com/2009/03/obamas_sights_on_second_amendm.html

Nations can pass it, but for it to have domestic effect, it needs to pass the U.S. Senate by a two-thirds vote and that is not going to happen.[16]

But as we have found out in the past four years since President Obama has been in office, you must listen carefully as to what Mr. Obama says, because he says one thing and then does another. President Obama also said the right of lawful citizens to carry a concealed firearm for personal protection should be banned nationwide.

American citizens have had the constitutional right to bear arms since the founding of our nation. No law-abiding American should ever be forced to give up this right. Since the beginning of Barack Obama's term in office, he has consistently tried to do away with our First and Second Amendment Rights and in many ways he has been successful. Now he is in office for a second term and he is gung-ho to rid America of her guns. What is not mentioned is that every Congressman probably has a concealed carry permit and the president is surrounded by secret servicemen that have concealed carry permits.

Since Mr. Obama's first day in office, he began attacking the rights of America's gun owners. This Administration loathes our First and Second Amendment rights, and will not give up on attempting to destroy these rights.

We now have had the tragedy in Newtown, Connecticut where all of these children were slain. Many are blaming this on the fact that handguns were used instead of putting the blame on the fact that this young 20 year old boy was mentally disturbed and should have been receiving help for his illness, and the fact that his mother should have had her guns under lock and key. We sometimes look to the wrong places to affix the blame when something goes wrong. It is so much easier to just blame guns.

You know, standing in the middle of a garage does not make you a car, but for some reason an anti-gun zealot just cannot get it through their head that a real person killed these children, not a gun. It could just as well have been Molotov cocktail, but this was the weapon this young lad got his hands on that terrible day. When a gang member cannot afford to buy a gun, he makes a zip gun, so

---

16   http://www.foxnews.com/world/2011/08/05/proposed-un-treaty-to-regu-late-global-firearms-trade-raising-concerns-for-us/#ixzz1wetLnygB

what good will it do to ban guns. Gangs are well armed and always will be. They smuggle their arms into the country just like drugs. Laws will not affect them. If a crazy cannot get his hands on a gun, he will build a bomb or a Molotov cocktail. You can learn how to build a bomb on the internet.

There is always a way to create havoc or to kill if that is what you are setting out to do. To use this massacre of little children to advance a premeditated, pre-existing political agenda that would not have saved those children is disgusting. The Second Amendment to the Constitution is a basic right of free people and will not be slashed by the executive power of this president.

There is no greater freedom than to own a firearm to protect yourself, your family, your community, and your nation. Thus, Second Amendment freedom is truly the heart and soul of America. (Speech by Wayne LaPierre, NRA Executive Vice President)

Mr. LaPierre clearly sees through Barack Obama's conspiracy to deceive voters and hide his true intentions to destroy the Second Amendment during his Second Term. I have previously set forth the many ways Barack Obama has set out to destroy this country in my book "Soundoff."

Barack Obama has already endorsed a total ban on manufacture, sale and possession of all handguns. Why? Because the law says if a gun is made in a state and is sold in the state then the Federal government has no control over it. Obama wants the control and power over us.

If we do not find better Congressmen to fight for us in Washington, we are going to end up like Europe. A number of states are passing laws that use the Tenth Amendment to curb Federal control. Their law says that "if a gun is made in the state and sold in the state, that the Federal government has no control over it." Obama endorsed a ban on the sale or transfer of all semi-automatic firearms.

He backed a 500 percent increase in Federal taxes on guns and ammunition.

He voted to ban single-shot, over-under, and side-by-side shotguns.

He said the right of lawful citizens to carry a firearm for personal protection should be banned nationwide.

He supported efforts to prohibit Americans from keeping a gun in their homes for self-defense.

Barack Obama appointed two justices to the United States Supreme Court, Sonia Sotomayor and Elena Kagan, who are two of the most obvious anti-gun justices in U. S. History.

To take a quote from Mr. LaPierrre's speech, "They've joined Justice Ruth Bader Ginsburg on the Court. Not long after hugging Obama like a giddy schoolgirl at the State of the Union, Ginsburg said this about our American Constitution, and I'm quoting her here: "I would not look to the U.S. Constitution if I were drafting a constitution in the year 2012. I might look at the Constitution of South Africa."

Let me quote her again: "I would not look to the U. S. Constitution if I were drafting a Constitution in the year 2012. I might look at the Constitution of South Africa."

So much for Justice Ginsburg's oath to uphold and defend our Constitution.

During Obama's second term, he will likely appoint one— perhaps three—more Supreme Court justices. If we get one more like those three, the Second Amendment is finished. It will be the end of our freedom forever for he is totally obsessed with doing away with our Second Amendment and any other rights that he cannot control. That is a fact.

The realities that we face today is that the President goes around Congress to impose any restrictions that he can on the Right to Keep and Bear Arms. He is already pushing the limits of executive order power, circumventing Congress with backdoor gun registration on lawful firearm purchases. And we know there are more executive orders ready to go, amounting to a full-scale regulatory war on the gun rights of every lawful American.

He hopes we will ignore those facts and that all gun owners will follow the media who denies them. This President is a total failure. He is doing everything he can possibly do to destroy this country. He is doing everything he can do to make this a socialist country. Socialism and Capitalism do not work together. Socialism works in Europe, not in America. Anyone that wants Socialism needs to move to Europe or Asia. You are not welcome in America. Get out of America!

"We deserve a president who truly shares our values and freedoms, guaranteed by the Bill of Rights, endowed by our Creator and due all humankind.

"Our liberty lives in the Second Amendment, the fundamental right that separates us from all other nations on earth. That freedom makes us better than other countries. That freedom makes us stronger. This President does not understand this right." Excerpts from speech of Wayne LaPierre of NRA)

The United States reversed policy and said it would back launching talks on a treaty to regulate arms sales as long as the talks operated by consensus, a stance critics said gave every nation a veto. The decision, announced in a statement released by the U.S. State Department, overturns the position of former President George W. Bush's administration, which had opposed such a treaty on the grounds that national controls were better. Obama Took the First Major Step in a Plan to Ban All Firearms in the United States.

The Obama administration intends to force gun control and a complete ban on all weapons for U.S. citizens through the signing of international treaties with foreign nations. By signing international treaties on gun control, the Obama administration can use the U.S. State Department to bypass the normal legislative process in Congress. Once the U.S. Government signs these international treaties, all US citizens will be subject to those gun laws created by foreign governments. These are laws that have been developed and promoted by organizations such as the United Nations and individuals such as George Soros and Michael Bloomberg. The laws are designed and intended to lead to the complete ban and confiscation of all firearms.

In 1929, the Soviet Union established gun control. From 1929 to 1953, about 20 million dissidents, unable to defend themselves, were founded up and exterminated.

In 1911, Turkey established gun control. From 1915 to 1917, 1.5 million Armenians, unable to defend themselves, were rounded up and exterminated.

Germany established gun control in 1938 and from 1939 to 1945, a total of 13 million Jews and others who were unable to defend themselves were rounded up and exterminated.

China established gun control in 1935. From 1948 to 1952, 20 million political dissidents, unable to defend themselves, were rounded up and exterminated.

Guatemala established gun control in 1964. From 1964 to 1981, 100,000 Mayan Indians, unable to defend themselves, were rounded up and exterminated.

Uganda established gun control in 1970. From 1971 to 1979, 300,000 Christians, unable to defend themselves, were rounded up and exterminated.

Australian citizens were forced to turn in their firearms and were promised protection. Armed robberies increased by 69%, assaults involving guns increased by 28%, gun murders increased by 19% and home invasions increased by 21%. The program did not work.

Cambodia established gun control in 1956. From 1975 to 1977, one million educated people, unable to defend themselves, were rounded up and exterminated.

Great Britain banned guns and at the present time their crime rate is nearly four times that of the United States. The UK has over 2,000 crimes recorded per 100,000 population making it the most violent place in Europe. In comparison, the U.S. has an estimated rate of 466 violent crimes recorded per 100,000 population. FBI data shows that 323 murders were committed with rifles of any kind in 2011. In comparison, 496 murders were committed with hammers and clubs, and 1,694 murders were perpetrated with knives.

I give CNN's Piers Morgan credit for having interviews where he can get in someone face because he is definitely a far left liberal. Frankly, I think he should be deported back to Europe, but this is still a free country. His views are more in line with MSNBC than what you would usually find on CNN. He is very hostile towards out Second Amendment and all gun owners and calls our Constitution "Our Little Book," but says he knows what is in it. Perhaps that is why he is hostile.

During WWII, the Japanese decided not to invade the United States because they knew most Americans were armed. Guns in the hands of honest citizens saves lives and property. Gun control adversely affects only the law abiding citizens.

Why carry a Gun?

My old grandpa said to me 'Son, there comes a time in every man's life when he stops bustin' knuckles and starts bustin' caps and usually it's when he becomes too old to take a butt whoopin.'

I don't carry a gun to kill people. I carry a gun to keep from being killed.

I don't carry a gun to scare people. I carry a gun because sometimes this world can be a scary place.

I don't carry a gun because I'm paranoid. I carry a gun because there are real threats in the world.

I don't carry a gun because I'm evil. I carry a gun because I have lived long enough to see the evil in the world.

I don't carry a gun because I hate the government. I carry a gun because I understand the limitations of government.

I don't carry a gun because I'm angry. I carry a gun so that I don't have to spend the rest of my life hating myself for failing to be prepared.

I don't carry a gun because I want to shoot someone. I carry a gun because I want to die at a ripe old age in my bed, and not on a sidewalk somewhere tomorrow afternoon.

I don't carry a gun because I'm a cowboy. I carry a gun because, when I die and go to heaven, I want to be a cowboy.

I don't carry a gun to make me feel like a man. I carry a gun because men know how to take care of themselves and the ones they love.

I don't carry a gun because I feel inadequate. I carry a gun because unarmed and facing three armed thugs, I am inadequate.

I don't carry a gun because I love it. I carry a gun because I love life and the people who make it meaningful to me.

Police protection is an oxymoron. Free citizens must protect themselves.

Police do not protect you from crime, they usually just investigate the crime after it happens and then call someone in to clean up the mess.

Personally, I carry a gun because I'm too young to die and too old to take a butt whoopin'.....author unknown (but obviously brilliant)'

Dianne Feinstein has proposed a Bill that will effectively take away our Second Amendment rights. As a matter of fact, she can be said to be dedicated to eliminating the Second Amendment. The California Democrat was one of the sponsors of the so-called "Brady Bill," the 1995 "assault weapons" ban. Faced with the limitations placed in the version that was making its way through Congress, Feinstein said, "If I could have gotten 51 votes in the Senate of the United States, for an outright ban, picking up every gun in America, Mr. and Mrs. America, turn 'em all in." Will someone please remind her of the Dick Act of 1902 and the United States Supreme Court Decision decided in 2008 of District of Columbia et al vs. Heller wherein the U. S. Supreme Court upheld our Second Amendment rights.[17]

Among her demands is that every gun owner must register every gun that you have. We all know that the purpose of having a national gun registry is the first step to confiscating every firearm in America. We are not talking about just some guns, but every gun. Her Bill does not talk about size or brand of semi-automatic guns. In her Bill, if your gun is black, and if you can grip it, it is banned.

Feinstein goes on to say "The time has come, America, to step up and ban these weapons. The other very important part of this bill is to ban large capacity ammunition feeding devices, those that hold more than 10 rounds. We have federal regulations and state laws that prohibit hunting ducks with more than three rounds. And yet it's legal to hunt humans with 15-round, 30-round, even 150-round magazines. Limiting magazine capacity is critical because it is when a criminal, a drug dealer, a deranged individual has to pause to change magazines and reload that the police or brave bystanders have the opportunity to take that individual down."[18]

---

[17]　http://libertypost.org/cgi-in/readart.cgi?ArtNum=329262
　　　http://www.scotusblog. com/wp-content/uploads/2008/06/07-2901.pdf
[18]　http://conservativebyte.com/2013/03/dianne-feinstein-its-legal-to-hunt-humans/#ixzz2N9ufgjw2

We all have a moral duty to protect our Second Amendment rights. We have freedoms in America that no other country has and the powers that be are trying to take them away from us. Our fore-fathers gave us a Constitution and Bill of Rights to protect us and it is up to us to fight to keep those freedoms and to make sure they are available to our children.

Do you want to be sitting in your rocking chair telling your grandkids about the good old days when you could go hunting or go to the range and fire any kind of gun you wanted to and you could take your grandson to the range with you, or do you want to be sitting in your rocking chair just telling your grandkids about the good old days that were and no longer are.

Fighting for freedom is often risky and chancy.

The Brady Bill was enacted in 1993 and since that time when you want to purchase a handgun, you have to fill out a form and there is a waiting period. It is the most important piece of Federal legislation as far as gun control, but a study by a Duke University Professor has shown that in recent decades there has been no statistically discernible effect on reducing gun deaths. The Professor, who acknowledged his personal sympathies were for gun control, said the real problem is the unregulated sales such as gun shows and no one knows how many guns are purchased with false ID's or exchanged privately, to say nothing of those being stolen.

The professor praised an Illinois law that requires gun owners to have ID cards and to record the ID numbers of individuals they sell guns to. Failure to keep records or report a stolen gun can result in prosecution. He also endorsed gun locks as a cheap and sensible way to render guns useless except to the owner.

Not everyone is afraid of Congress. Sheriff Richard Mack of the State of Arizona did not like the Brady Bill and he decided to do something about it. "I have met thousands of concerned patriotic Americans, and one thing has remained constant," Sheriff Richard Mack of Graham County, Arizona noted, "the people of this great country are afraid! Afraid of big government, afraid of losing their lands and homes to ruthless tax collectors, afraid of losing their children to bureaucrats who disapprove of spanking, and most of all, afraid of having their God-given rights and freedoms trampled by the very servants charged with protecting them."

Passed by Congress and signed by President Clinton in 1993, the Brady Act imposes a five-day waiting period on handgun purchasers. It also requires local law enforcement officials to check prospective buyers' backgrounds to determine whether they are forbidden to own guns for various reasons, such as being convicted felons, mental illness or subject to domestic violence restraining orders. Mack filed a lawsuit against the Federal government in the United States District Court for the District of Arizona in which he challenged the constitutionality of the Brady Bill gun control act. Judge John Roll of Tucson agreed. The issue was considered by the U.S. Supreme Court in the Fall Term.[19]

I am for what will make the job of our peace officers easier to catch the criminals in our society, but it has already been proven that gun control is not the answer. Guns do not kill people. People kill people. There has been a big push for gun control since the killing of all of the children in Connecticut. It was a horrendous crime. No one disputes that. You cannot blame it on guns. You must blame it on a young man that was mentally ill and his mother that knew he was mentally ill and did not seek help for him. Put the blame and responsibility where it belongs and not on every responsible person in the nation that owns a gun.

If you want some statistics, take a look at some from the United States Department of Health & Human Services. They say there are 700,000 doctors in the United States. They also say that there are 120,000 accidental deaths caused by physicians per year. The statistic for accidental deaths per physician is 17.14%.

---

[19] http://search.mywebsearch.com/mywebsearch/redirect.jhtml?search-for=Sheriff+defending+under+Brady+Gun+Control+Bill&cb=X-M&p2=%5EXM%5Exdm003%5EYYY%5Eus&qid=18f013ffadf343a-fa1161f526f4c1dc7&n=77DE8857&ptb=42750FF0-673C-4BC7-8BD8-3118294B01B&si=CMuP4Mvei7QCFaN_hp&qs=&pr=GG&tpr=hst&re-direct=mPWsrdz9heamc8iHEhldER%2FfmAGmpBat35ZhBJUS2WpJ-cynyeDFOyG83qkhqlA%2BHDDK10k9HBbk5qTKm6%2BFTF1ClIFX-UIEnKuRipISnHdR0%3D&ord=2&ct=AR&

Now let's look at the statistics for guns put out by the FBI. The FBI says that the number of gun owners in the United States is 80,000,000. (yes! That is 80 million). They also say that the number of accidental deaths by a gun per year, by all age groups, is 1,500. So, that would make the number of accidental deaths per gun owner at 0.001875%. Now why is it again that everyone is going after the gun owners?

Or, let us look at it this way: In the year 2011, there were 323 people killed by an AR-15 rifles. There were 496 people killed by a common household hammer. There were 650 people killed by knives. There were 12,000 people killed by drunk drivers. There were 195,000 people killed by medical malpractice. You are 600 times more likely to die from ObamaCare than by an AR-15 rifle. Illinois does not want gun control, but they keep electing democrats in their State Legislature and to represent them in the Federal government.

The Democratic Legislature are pushing through gun legislation where the Senate committee approved two bills, one dealing with weapons and the other with magazines. Democratic supporters will face a tough sell in the full Senate. One measure would ban the possession, delivery, sale and transfer of semi-automatic handguns and rifles. People who currently own such weapons could keep them but would have to register them. The bill would allow semi-automatic weapons to be used at shooting ranges, but those facilities would be regulated. When laws are passed, it is the law abiding citizens that abide by the laws, not the criminals.

A National Rifle Association lobbyist told lawmakers the bill would restrict about 75 percent of handguns and 50 percent of long guns in circulation today. He also said it would treat law-abiding gun owners like criminals and is in conflict with Second Amendment rights upheld by the courts. He said, "I've never seen a piece of legislation that tramples on so many court decisions."

The other bill, introduced by Democratic State Sen. Dan Kotowski, would limit ammunition magazines to 10 or fewer rounds.[20]

---

[20]   http://www.foxnews.com/politics/2013/01/02/illinois-dems-press-forward-with-gun-control-bills-firearms-group-warns-no/#ixzz2GwibUYYc

As long as the people of Illinois sit back and do nothing, these legislators will run over them. They need to get on the telephones and contact these legislators and let them know they are not in agreement with what they are doing, and they need to sign petitions contrary to what is going on. Sitting back and doing nothing is affecting their Second Amendment rights and no one is fighting for them. This is all about total power over the people. The government hates guns in the hands of people that can think for themselves and do not obey without question.

It used to be that when a President retired, he and his family were protected by the Secret Service for a period of ten years.

Even though Obama is fighting to have your gun rights taken away from you, he just signed a Bill that all Presidents, past, present and future, and their families, will have lifetime Secret Service Protection. Naturally, all Secret Service agents carry guns, but that is okay.

From now on, the Obama Administration and Media will be playing every psychological weapons game on the American public they can come up with. They will make it their agenda and goal to see that all future generations are ashamed to own a gun. They will continuously use the term "assault weapons" instead of semi-automatic rifles. That way they can question whether you go hunting with a rifle or an "assault weapon." That term did not exist until someone made it up in 1988. The truth is, there is no such word; it is a political term developed by anti-gun advocates. It is another term for an "assault rifle." Myself, I prefer to call them "defense weapons."

An AR-15 is a semi-automatic assault rifle that fires one round each time the trigger is pulled. The government is calling them "assault weapons." The truth is they operate the same as a "ranch rifle." You shoot one round at a time. They operate just like a shotgun. You shoot one round at a time. They shoot just like a pistol. You shoot one round at a time. They shoot just like a double action revolver. You shoot one round at a time. The confusion is its perception. It looks different. It looks menacing. As soon as it was manufactured, the anti-gun lobby began comparing it to a machine gun, which it is not, and the media followed suit. Then they campaigned to have it banned when it is only a different looking rifle. Homeland Security is presently buying up every AR-15 and matching 30 round clips that they can get their hands on. It is just us commoners that they do not want to have this gun. Who is the one that is getting ready for war?

The nice thing about the AR-15 is it can easily be converted to a muzzle loader for black powder, a crossbow for archery hunting, an air rifle, and can be adapted to fire over a dozen different rifle and pistol calibers. The design makes it easy to install optics and scopes, and the collapsible stock allows the length to be adjusted so different statured shooters can comfortably use the same rifle. All of these features are why it is so popular.

The Media intentionally published the names and addresses of gun owners in the same manner as if they were sex offenders. What it intentionally did was make the people vulnerable to someone breaking into their home that was looking for a weapon. And the government's next campaign will be you really do not need a handgun either because you cannot shoot a deer with a handgun, can you?

Then there is the new one where your mental health professional is now required to ask you if you own a gun and if you say yes, your doctor is required to report you. This raises the question of presumption of confidentiality that has been inherent in mental health treatment. The possibility of being reported to the authorities, even if they do not have a weapon, may be enough to dissuade a patient from seeking treatment or from being honest about their compulsions. The good thing is you are not required to give an answer, so if you wish, just say "stick it," or nothing at all.

Another new agenda being pursued by our government is talk in the gun control circles of subverting the Second Amendment through the back door by commissioning the Center for Disease Control to study gun violence. The object is to have the Center for Disease Control to find gun deaths an epidemic and find a way to declare gun deaths a disease. Once the U.S. Government declares gun deaths to be a disease it will have the authority to deal with it much like any other disease, with wide latitude. Keep in mind as ObamaCare gets implemented this issue will creep into government health care and be dealt with as a health issue. They will erode the Second Amendment piece by piece no matter how long it takes in their mind. They are relentless. The executive actions could include giving the Centers for Disease Control and Prevention authority to conduct national research on guns, more aggressive enforcement of existing gun laws and pushing for wider sharing of existing gun databases among Federal and state agencies, members of Congress in the meeting said.[21]

Remember when you were a little kid and all you had to do was run around outside the house and play games with your siblings or your friends? A couple of those games were either cops and robbers or cowboys and Indians. If we were lucky, we even had a toy gun. If we did not have a gun, we used our fingers. Maybe we even had a water gun and we would squirt each other with water. But we never dreamed of killing each other or a classmate in school for real. The idea of having a toy gun was that it was a cap gun and it made a noise, not to shoot someone for real. If we came from a poor family, we could not afford caps for the toy gun and we would just point it and say, "Pow, pow." If we were shot we would fall on the ground giggling because it was a game all in fun and we would not dream of touching dad's real guns. Dad used those for hunting. What do you think we are; some kind of a nut?

We were taught right and wrong because we were raised in church. Our classmates in school were right there in church beside us and most of them were also our best friends. God was also allowed in our schools back then. Every morning the first thing we did before class began was to say the Pledge of Allegiance to the flag and it had the words "under God" in it and it meant something. We were not afraid to pray in school or mention the word God for fear of offending someone. Even the Democrats believed in God. Now, it is different. Recently two 6-year-old boys were suspended from school for playing cops and robbers during recess because they were using their fingers to make an imaginary gun and saying "pow." The school had to overturn the suspension, of course, after the parents had to go to

---

21   http://www.politico.com/story/2013/01/biden-guns-executive-actions-86187. html?hp=t1_3

the expense of getting an attorney to appeal the decision. The principal wrote a letter to the one parent stating that their son threatened to shoot another student.

Who is really the paranoid ones in this country? Is it the gun zealots, or the legal gun owners? We are naïve if we think that oppression will never happen here as it has in other countries.[22]

When you have a mentally disturbed man or child holding a gun, no gun law can save a person from their terror.

Does this government really think that 312 million inhabitants of the United States are willingly going to give up every gun they own to the United States government just because the United States Congress and the President says so when our Constitution guarantees us the right to bear arms?

The Brady Handgun Violence Prevention Act already requires Federal background checks for gun purchases, but not every firearm sale is covered under the law.

Currently, law enforcement agencies cannot perform a NICS check when transferring, returning or selling weapons that have been confiscated, seized or recovered. The new rules would change that, allowing officials to perform a background check on people who receive those weapons to ensure that they are permitted to own a gun.

Obama ordered the rule change in a January 16 memo that called for "rulemaking to give law enforcement the ability to run a full background check on an individual before returning a seized gun."

Holder is also proposing that the NICS hold on to records of denied weapon sales that are more than 10 years old. When the NICS was established, the Justice Department ordered that the records be moved to a storage facility after 10 years, which Holder says is no longer necessary.

"The FBI has therefore determined that for NICS' own internal business operations, litigation and prosecution purposes, and proper administration of the system; NICS shall retain denied transaction records on site." "The retention of denied transaction information ... will enhance the efficiency and operational capability of the NICS."

---

[22] http://politicaloutcast.com/2013/01/two-first-graders-suspended-for-playing-cops-robbers/#ixzz2IS6wXltu

The proposed rules would also give Native American tribes access to NICS. Currently, only Federal, state, or local agencies can perform the checks, which leaves out "domestic dependent nations" recognized by the United States.

The Justice Department is not the only part of the administration that has been asked to take action in response to last month's school shooting in Newtown, Conn. The president has also ordered the Department of Health and Human Services, the Department of Education and the Centers for Disease Control (CDC) to get involved.

One of Obama's directives was to ensure coverage of mental health treatment in Medicaid and under the healthcare reform law. He also ordered increased training of school staff to help them recognize signs of mental illness.

The CDC, meanwhile, was directed to study the causes of gun violence. The president urged Congress to approve $10 million for the agency to examine whether there are links between shooting sprees and violent entertainment. Comments on the Justice Department proposals are due by March 28.[23]

Now if you really want to get into something interesting, go to Harvard Law School, where most brilliance is borne. Professor Einer Elhauge, said "Now I will show you where the Constitution grants authority to Congress to require adult citizens to get armed! The Constitution Authorizes Congress To Require Citizens to Buy Guns and Ammunition.

In 1792, Congress passed "An Act more effectually to provide for the National Defense by establishing an Uniform Militia throughout the United States".2 This Act required all able-bodied male citizens (except for Federal officers and employees) between the ages of 18 and under 45 to enroll in their State Militia, get a gun and ammunition, and train.

Does Congress have authority in the Constitution to require this? Yes! Article I, Sec. 8, clause 16 says Congress has the Power: "To provide for organizing, arming, and disciplining, the Militia, and for governing such Part of them as may be employed in the Service of the

---

23 http://thehill.com/blogs/regwatch/pending-regs/279345-holder-begins-gun-control-push

United States, reserving to the States respectively, the Appointment of the Officers, and the Authority of training the Militia according to the discipline prescribed by Congress;"

That is what authorizes Congress to require adult male citizens to buy guns and ammunition.

As Section 1 of the Militia Act of 1792 reflects, the "Militia" is the citizenry! Our Framers thought it such a fine idea that The People be armed, that they required it by law! See, e.g., the second half of Federalist Paper No. 46 where James Madison, Father of Our Constitution, speaks of how wonderful it is that the American People are armed – and why they need to be.

So! In the case of Congress' requiring adult citizens to buy guns and ammunition, Congress has specific authority under Art. I, Sec. 8, cl.16.[24]

Every change that is made, every law that Congress comes up with, every Executive Order that Obama signs, eats away at a little more of our Second Amendment rights. Are we going to keep letting them get a little more foot hold each time until we no longer have any of those rights? That is what is happening.

---

[24] http://freedomoutpost.com/2013/02/why-congress-may-lawfully-require-cit-izens-to-buy-guns-ammunition-but-not-to-submit-to-obamacare/#ixzz2K-oGWFFdZ

VII

Obama's Record

O nly in America can a man with no background, no qualifications and no experience ... and a complete failure at his job ... get reelected.

How can so many citizens be so blind and keep saying give him a chance? How can so many citizens keep saying the economy is growing when it is failing? How can so many citizens keep saying unemployment is decreasing when it is only that people have given up looking for work? That is why Obama keeps working the public. He has to keep dazzling the public; mesmerizing his populace and work his magic on the one hand, so he can do his dirty deeds behind your back with the other. He talks about transparency, but there has never been transparency in this presidency. Everything he talks about is spending your money and "I am going to do this" and that means an Executive Order. Despite Barack Obama's rhetoric, he had a propensity to say and do anything to get elected. While in the Illinois Legislature, he voted four times to allow criminal charges against homeowners who defended their person and home with a gun.

In fact, Barack Obama specifically voted four times in the Illinois Legislature to allow criminal charges against a homeowner who used a firearm in self-defense of their person and home —

specifically what the Supreme Court says is a constitutional right. Obama may say he supports the constitution, but his record says exactly the opposite.

Mr. Obama said "I believe that the Constitution confers an individual right to bear arms. But just because you have an individual right does not mean that the state or local government can't constrain the exercise of that right."

Justice Kagan's threat to Gun owners

The Washington Times says the nominee has a past that is opposed to individual self-defense.

Obama poses a real and present danger to the Second Amendment, and he is working to pack the Supreme Court with justices who will undermine Americans' gun rights.

Obama did not fess up to this radical agenda when running for the highest office in the land. "I have said consistently that I believe that the Second Amendment is an individual right, and that was the essential decision that the Supreme Court came down on," Obama told Fox News in June 2008. Despite the campaign rhetoric, Obama is appointing judges who strongly oppose that position. The most recent pick, Elena Kagan, ran much of Clinton's war on guns from 1995 to 1999.

When Kagan served as Clinton's deputy domestic policy adviser, she was a feverish proponent of gun control. From gunlock mandates to gun-show regulations, she was instrumental in pushing anti-gun policies, according to the Los Angeles Times. Every court nomination counts. Two years ago, the Supreme Court barely mustered a narrow 5-4 majority to strike down the extreme District of Columbia gun ban. Should Justice Anthony Kennedy or one of the four more conservative justices retire or die while Obama is in office, the high court likely will undo such narrow victories for the Second Amendment. While Kagan was nominated to replace the liberal Justice, John Paul Stevens, and thus will not swing the court in a new direction, her being there will necessitate that gun owners concentrate more than ever on fighting outright gun bans.

Kagan's defenders acknowledge her liberal political views but claim that as a judge, the former Harvard Law School dean will somehow manage to separate her judgments from her political opinions. The problem is that her legal views correspond with her political views. When Kagan clerked for Justice Thurgood Marshall, she wrote, "I'm not sympathetic" to the claim that "the District of Columbia's firearms statutes violate [an individual's] constitutional right to 'keep and bear Arms.'"

Kagan is Justice Sonia Sotomayor's soul sister when it comes to gun control. Last year, during her confirmation hearings, Sotomayor insisted the Supreme Court had never found that an individual right to self-defense exists. Two of Justice Sotomayor's own appeals court decisions came to the same conclusion. One ruling denied there is an individual right to self-defense. In another case, even after the Supreme Court struck down the District's gun ban, Judge Sotomayor opined that any restrictions on self-defense would pass constitutional muster so long as politicians who passed it said they had a good reason.

Senators must realize that a vote for Kagan for the Supreme Court is another vote against gun rights.[25]

Gun rights extended by Supreme court

The Washington Post is reporting The Supreme Court held that Americans have the right to own a gun for self-defense anywhere they live, advancing a recent trend by the John Roberts-led bench to embrace gun rights.

By a 5-4 vote, the justices cast doubt on handgun bans in the Chicago area, but signaled that some limitations on the Constitution's "right to keep and bear arms" could survive legal challenges.

Justice Samuel Alito, writing for the court, said that the Second Amendment right "applies equally to the Federal government and the states."

The court was split along familiar ideological lines, with five conservative-moderate justices in favor of gun rights and four liberals opposed. Chief Justice Roberts voted with the majority. Two

---

[25]   http://www.washingtontimes.com/news/2010/jun/9/kagans-threat-to-gun-owners/

years ago, the court declared that the Second Amendment protects an individual's right to possess guns, at least for purposes *of self-defense in the home.*

That ruling applied only to Federal laws. It struck down a ban on handguns and a trigger lock requirement for other guns in the District of Columbia, a Federal city with unique legal standing. At the same time, the court was careful not to cast doubt on other regulations of firearms here.

Gun rights proponents almost immediately filed a Federal lawsuit challenging gun control laws in Chicago and its suburb of Oak Park, Illinois, where handguns have been banned for nearly 30 years. The Brady Center to Prevent Gun Violence says those laws appear to be the last two remaining outright bans.

Lower Federal courts upheld the two laws, noting that judges on those benches were bound by Supreme Court precedent and that it would be up to the high court justices to ultimately rule on the true reach of the Second Amendment.

The Supreme Court already has said that most of the guarantees in the Bill of Rights serve as a check on state and local, as well as Federal, laws.

Obama advocates for "common Sense" Gun control

Matt Schneider says, that on a smaller platform than some may have hoped, Obama wrote an op-ed in the Arizona Daily Star launching his intention to tackle serious and "common sense" gun control. Two months after the Tucson, Arizona shooting tragedy, Obama seems to be searching for middle ground on the issue in an effort to protect "our children's futures."

Obama first reaffirmed he has no intention of confiscating guns, calling for more stringent enforcement of existing gun laws, citing the "awful consequences" of gun violence in American society.

Obama says legislation to bolster criminal background checks for gun buyers hasn't been properly implemented, with too many states providing "incomplete and inadequate" information. He says the system needs to be "faster and nimbler" so it works for gun sellers and "criminals can't escape it."

Now, like the majority of Americans, I believe that the Second Amendment guarantees an individual right to bear arms....And, in fact, my administration has not curtailed the rights of gun owners — it has expanded them, including allowing people to carry their guns in national parks and wildlife refuges.

And Obama discussed his awareness of how difficult it will be to approach an issue that both sides feel so passionately about:

"I know that every time we try to talk about guns, it can reinforce stark divides. People shout at one another, which makes it impossible to listen. We mire ourselves in stalemate, which makes it impossible to get to where we need to go as a country." Then Obama outlined a few practical beginning steps, including "enforcing laws that are already on the books," strengthening the National Instant Criminal Background Check System, rewarding states that provide the best data, and making the background check system "faster and nimbler" so that criminals can't escape it. Concluding, Obama stated, "I want this to at least be the beginning of a new discussion on how we can keep America safe for all our people." Given that NRA supporters often fear any increased Federal gun control legislation could be a slippery slope towards greater restrictions in the future, and given that anti-gun activists will likely think Obama's first steps here don't go far enough, it's likely many will be eager to participate in the "new discussion" Obama is starting.

Obama says one thing, but . . .

Obama Plans changes to Gun Policy

Sam Stein says the Obama administration has conducted informal discussions with groups from both ends of the gun-policy spectrum, including law enforcement and gun-rights organizations, and is set to hold formal meetings in an effort to chart out a set of new firearms policies, administration officials say.

Spearheaded by the Department of Justice, the talks were described by one individual involved in the discussions as a "feeling-out process." With more official meetings set to provide the clearest indication that the White House is readying a response to the shooting of Rep. Gabrielle Giffords (D-Ariz.) and 19 others at Tucson in early January.

"As the president said, we should focus on sound, effective steps that will keep guns out of the hands of the criminals, fugitives, people with serious mental illness, and others who have no business possessing a gun and who are prohibited by laws on the books from owning a gun," Justice Department spokesman Matthew Miller said. "We will be meeting with stakeholders on all sides of the issue to discuss how we can find sensible, intelligent ways to make the country safer."

The goal is to finalize a set of policy changes, including, perhaps, legislation that could pass through a Congress hostile to abridgments of Second Amendment rights. The last serious bite at the apple occurred following the shootings at Virginia Tech in April 2007.

In a Sunday op-ed for the Arizona Daily Star, President Barack Obama called for a three-pronged approach:enforcing the laws already on the books, including the National Instant Criminal Background Check System; pushing for greater state-to-state coordination; and expediting background checks and the release of relevant data.

The NRA response To Obama's op-ed on gun laws:

> On Sunday, March 13, the Arizona Star published an op-ed from President Barack Obama that discussed his belief that we should seek "agreement on gun reforms."

Those"agreements"would almost certainly include new restrictions on the Second Amendment rights of the American people that are unneeded and unacceptable for law-abiding gun owners.

It's interesting that Obama didn't ready a response to the murder of 13 and the wounding of 30 others at Fort Hood, but that terror attack doesn't fit Obama's narrative.

Obama looking For ways around congress on Gun Policy

Faced with a Congress hostile to even slight restrictions of Second Amendment rights, the Obama administration is exploring potential changes to gun laws that can be secured strictly through executive action, administration officials say.

The Department of Justice held the first in what is expected to be a series of meetings with a group of stakeholders in the ongoing gun-policy debates. Before the meeting, officials said part of the discussion was expected to center around the White House's options for shaping policy on its own or through its adjoining agencies and departments — on issues ranging from beefing up background checks to encouraging better data-sharing.

Administration officials said talk of executive orders or agency action are among a host of options that Barack Obama and his advisers are considering. "The purpose of these discussions is to be a productive exchange of good ideas from folks across the spectrum," one official said. "We think that's a good place to start." House Democrats joined New York City Mayor Michael Bloomberg to offer another possible starting point, announcing legislation that would make fundamental changes to the nation's gun background check system. Sponsored by Rep. Carolyn McCarthy (D-N.Y.), a longtime gun control advocate, the bill mirrors one introduced late last month by another New York Democrat, Sen. Chuck Schumer.

> "Too often, any serious discussion about guns devolves into ideological arguments that have nothing to do with the real problem," Bloomberg, a co-founder of the coalition Mayors against Illegal Guns, told reporters at a press event outside the Capitol. "Our coalition strongly believes in the Second Amendment. We also know from experience that we can keep guns away from dangerous people without imposing burdens on law-abiding gun owners."

For gun control advocates, however, executive action remains a more promising — albeit more limited — vehicle for reform than Congress. The Huffington Post first reported that the Justice Department was convening meetings with groups from across the ideological spectrum in an effort to chart potential policy changes to Second Amendment law.

"We need tougher laws, but there's a lot we can and should be doing to enforce the laws we have," said Mark Glaze, the executive director of Mayors against Illegal Guns. "Sometimes it's a question of manpower and money, but in many cases it's just a question of political will. We think the president knows that and is getting there."

The extent to which Obama can change the gun law without the hand of Congress is not, gun control activists say, wholly insignificant. Though they say they'd prefer longer-lasting, broader legislative responses to shootings like that which occurred in Tucson, Ariz., in early January, there are notable gaps that can be filled with presidential action.

What that official meant was, a productive exchange of good ideas from folks across the "anti-gun and gun control" spectrum.

"Under the radar"

David Codrea is reporting that anti-gun activist Sarah Brady claims Barack Obama is committed to stealth gun control according to a report in The Washington Post.

Recounting a March 30 meeting between Brady, her husband Jim and White House Press secretary Jay Carney, The Post reports:

> During the meeting, Obama dropped in and, according to Sarah Brady, brought up the issue of gun control, "to fill us in that it was very much on his agenda," she said.

> "I just want you to know that we are working on it," Brady recalled Obama telling them. "We have to go through a few processes, but under the radar."

Among the measures discussed:

[H]ow records get into the system and what can be done about firearms retailers. Her husband specifically brought up the proposed ban on large magazine clips…

While Brady reports Obama "just laughed," she also expressed "absolute confidence that the president was committed to regulation." That Obama is coyly discussing "processes…under the radar" directly contradicts a campaign pledge further documented via an official White House memorandum:

My Administration is committed to creating an unprecedented level of openness in Government. We will work together to ensure the public trust and establish a system of transparency, public participation, and collaboration. Openness will strengthen our democracy and promote efficiency and effectiveness in Government. There is nothing transparent, open or participatory about maneuvers to exercise control over unalienable rights. The entire ***purpose of being "under the radar" is to escape detection.***

For the administration to continue an "under the radar" gun policy points to directed practices very different from its public promises. But it does give insight into how another stealth program, "Project Gunwalker," was allowed and encouraged, and why accusations of stonewalling continue to be made by both Senate and House investigators.

When Barack Obama claimed that Illinois sportsmen know him as an advocate for their rights, the Illinois State Rifle Association (ISRA) released the following statement:

"One of the most blatant lies ever to come from a politician's mouth. Any sportsman who counts Barack Obama as one of his friends is seriously confused."

> "Throughout his tenure in the Illinois Senate, Obama served as one of the most loyal foot soldiers in Mayor Daley's campaign to abolish civilian firearm ownership. While a state senator, Obama voted for legislation that would ban and forcibly confiscate nearly every shotgun, target rifle and hunting rifle in

the state. Obama also voted for bills that would ration the number of firearms a law-abiding citizen could own, yet give a pass to the violent thugs who roam our streets. And, inexplicably, Obama voted four times against legislation that would allow citizens to use firearms to defend their homes and families."

"Let us also not forget that Obama served as a director of the Joyce Foundation. While on the Joyce Foundation board, Obama funneled tens of millions of dollars to radical gun control organizations such as the Illinois Council against Handgun Violence and the Violence Policy Center."

And Barack Obama specifically voted four times in the Illinois Legislature to allow criminal charges against a homeowner who used a firearm in self-defense of their person and home — specifically what the Supreme Court says is a constitutional right. Obama may say he supports the Second Amendment, but he's lying (again) — his record says exactly the opposite.

Obama: We're working on Gun Control "Under the Radar"

Fox Nation is reporting that On March 30, the 30th anniversary of the assassination attempt on President Ronald Reagan, Jim Brady, who sustained a debilitating head wound in the attack, and his wife, Sarah, came to Capitol Hill to push for a ban on the controversial "large magazines." Brady, for whom the law requiring background checks on handgun purchasers is named,then met with White House press secretary Jay Carney. During the meeting, Obama dropped in and, according to Sarah Brady, brought up the issue of gun control, "to fill us in that it was very much on his agenda," she said.

"I just want you to know that we are working on it," Brady recalled Obama telling them. "We have to go through a few processes, but under the radar."[26]

---

[26]   http://www.theobamafile.com/ politics/2ndAmendment.htm

III. President's campaign Strategy

The Obama Administration officials were deliberately keeping gun owners in the dark about the President's agenda on gun control as we head into the general election for 2012 because the Administration knew when gun owners and NRA members showed up at the polls en masse a candidate would lose. The Obama campaign strategy went something like this:

1. Pretend to be pro-gun or at least pushing a pro-gun agenda;
2. With gun owners neutralized, he will win the election and after he is re-elected, he will not have to answer to the voters because he will not have to face another election;
3. Launch a full scale assault to rip the Second Amendment out of the Bill of Rights through legislation, litigation, regulation, executive orders, international treaties, every level of power at his disposal.

He has loaded his administration with anti-gun extremists bent on destroying our Second Amendment freedoms.

With the help of his old Secretary of State, Hillary Clinton, Obama made the United States an active partner to the United Nations gun-ban treaty. The U.N. will unveil this unmitigated attack on our sovereignty this summer and the Obama administration has vowed to implement it.

Obama appointed two anti-Second Amendment Supreme Court justices and continues to flood our lower Federal Courts with dozens of anti-gun, activist judges.

With the help of his attorney general, Eric Holder, Obama led a campaign to demonize law-abiding gun owners, claiming our Second Amendment rights were to blame for drug violence in Mexico. And in fact, emails recently released by the Justice Department prove that operation "Fast and Furious" was a deliberate attempt to build the case for a gun-control agenda.

Obama unilaterally imposed gun registration in four border states — requiring gun dealers to register the sales of any law-abiding citizen who purchases more than one semi-automatic rifle within one week.[27]

IV.   What does he really think

So what are we to believe is Obama's position on gun owner-ship? He may tell campaign audiences that he believes in the right to own guns if that is what they want to hear. In the name of security, his idea of common sense regulation is making gun ownership com-pletely illegal. That is what the Washington D.C. ban is. No resident of Washington D.C. may possess a gun in his or her home. Does that tell you a thing or two about what he really thinks? But that has not stopped crime in Washington, D.C.

John R. Lott Jr., a senior research scientist at the University of Maryland and author of More Guns, Less Crime, argues that the city officials reasoning about eliminating the city f rom gun violence is flawed. He said after the law went into effect DC crime statistics shows gun violence increased not decreased.

"In the five years before Washington's ban in 1976, the murder rate fell from 37 to 27 per 100,000. In the five years after it went into effect, the murder rate rose back up to 35. But there is one fact that seems particularly hard to ignore. D.C.'s murder rate fluctuated after 1976 but has only once fallen below what it was in 1976 (that happened years later, in 1985). Does D.C. really want to argue that the gun ban reduced the murder rate?"

Lott also says crime rates soared in other cities like Chicago after guns were banned. But Mayor Emmanuel is not giving up. He is now going after the banks in Chicago that are financing gun makers, as if that is going to make any difference. The mayor is urging banks to stop lines of credit, financing for acquisitions and expansions and financial advising.

---

[27]   http://dailycaller.com/2011/12/12/the-obama-administration-is-planning-a-second-term-attack-on-gun-rights/#ixzz1tqo5LfIU

"Chicago has banned all handguns since 1982. Indeed, D.C. points to Chicago's ban to support its own ban. But, the gun ban didn't work at all when it came to reducing violence. Chicago's murder rate fell from 27 to 22 per 100,000 in the five years before the law and then rose slightly to 23. The change is even more dramatic when compared to five neighboring Illinois counties: Chicago's murder rate fell from being 8.1 times greater than its neighbors in 1977 to 5.5 times in 1982, and then went way up to 12 times greater in 1987."[28]

V.   Obama's budget

Another tell-tale sign of how the President feels about gun owners is to take a look at the national budget.

One provision that was put on the chopping block was a ban on the importation of shotguns deemed by the BATFE to be non-"sporting." Congress passed this to block an Obama administration plan to expand the use of the "sporting purposes" test once again, this time to ban the importation of many popular defensive, target shooting and hunting shotguns. Removing this provision is clearly a first step toward implementing a new import ban.

The other new provision for 2012 was a ban on the use of tax dollars to lobby for new gun laws. Obama signaled that he would take this step when he announced at the bill signing for the 2012 legislation that he and his administration would not be bound by that provision. And in his budget, Obama would get rid of that restriction entirely.

Another provision deleted was a prohibition on the use of funds for anti-gun research at the National Institutes of Health and the Centers for Disease Control. These prohibitions have been passed by Congress to stop these groups f rom funding junk science "studies" in support of new restrictions on gun rights.

Obama also wants to get rid of the provision that stops the Department of Defense from destroying surplus M1 Garands and M1 carbines—a provision that has been in place for over 30 years.

---

[28]   http://thestateofamerica.wordpress.com/2008/02/28/barak-obama-and-the-second-amendment/

And he wants to drop a provision that stops the destruction of spent military brass. Without these protections, thousands of surplus rifles could be destroyed instead of being sold to law-abiding Americans through the Civilian Marksmanship Program, and millions of recyclable brass cases will be melted down as scrap rather than being made available to reloaders.

There is good news for gun owners, though. No one—not even Obama or his closest allies—believe this budget will be passed, and it may not even be brought up for a vote.[29]

VI.

Without a doubt, Barack Obama has proven himself to be an enemy to the law abiding firearm owner. While a state senator, Barack Obama voted four times against legislation that would allow a homeowner to use a firearm in defense of home and family. Does that sound like he is your friend or your foe?

They say you can always judge a person by the company he keeps. Barack Obama has many strange friends; most of them socialists and Marxists and enemies of "The People." Among his so-called friends are the Rev. Michael Pfleger — a renegade Chicago priest who has openly called for the murder of gun shop owners and pro-gun legislators. Then there is his buddy Richard Daley, the ex-mayor of Chicago who has declared that if it were up to him, nobody would be allowed to own a gun. And then, of course, let's not forget Obama's close pal George Soros — the guy who has pumped millions of dollars into the UN's international effort to disarm law-abiding citizens and the man who is trying to purchase all gun manufacturing companies in America.

While a board member of the leftist Joyce Foundation, Barack Obama wrote checks for tens of millions of dollars to extremist gun control organizations such as the Illinois Council against Handgun Violence and the Violence Policy Center.

---

[29]　http://www.nraila.org/news-issues/articles/2012/on-the-second-amendment,-obama-budget-tells-all.aspx

During the 2008 primary, Barack Obama tried to hide behind tenuous statements of support for "sportsmen" and general support for the right to keep and bear arms. But his actual record, based on votes taken, political associations, and established positions, shows that Obama is a severe threat to our Second Amendment liberties.

Do not listen to his campaign rhetoric! Look instead to what he has said and done during his entire political career.

The fact is that Barack Obama opposed four of the five Supreme Court justices who affirmed an individual right to keep and bear arms. He voted against the confirmation of Justices Alito and Roberts and he has stated he would not have appointed Thomas or Scalia. (United States Senate vote 245, September 29, 2005 and vote 2, January 31, 2006 and Saddleback Forum, August 16, 2008.) The fact is that Barack Obama voted for an Illinois State Senate bill to ban and confiscate "assault weapons," but the bill was so poorly crafted, it would have also banned most semi-automatic and single and double barrel shotguns commonly used by sportsmen. (Illinois Senate Judiciary Committee, March 13, 2003. See the vote tally.[30]

The fact is that Barack Obama voted to allow reckless lawsuits designed to bankrupt the firearms industry. (United States Senate, 397, vote number 219, July 29, 2005.[31]

The fact is that Barack Obama wants to re-impose the failed and discredited Clinton Gun Ban. (Illinois Senate Debate #3: Barack Obama vs. Alan Keyes.[32]

The fact is that Barack Obama voted to ban almost all rifle ammunition commonly used for hunting and sport shooting. (United States Senate, S. 397, vote number 217, Kennedy amendment July 29, 2005.)[33]

The fact is that Barack Obama was a member of the Board of Directors of the Joyce Foundation, the leading source of funds

---

[30]   http://www.nrapvf.org/Media/pdf/sb1195_obama.pdf.

[31]   http://www.senate.gov/legislative/LIS/roll_call_lists/roll_call_vote_cfm.cfm?congress=1 09&session=1&vote=00219)

[32]   http://www.ontheissues.org/2008/Barack_Obama_Gun_ Control.htm.
        http://www.ontheissues.org/IL_2004_Senate_3rd.htm

[33]   http://www.senate.gov/legislative/LIS/roll_call_lists/roll_call_vote_cfm.
        cfm?Congress=109&session=1&vote=00217

for anti-gun organizations and "research." (1998 Joyce Foundation Annual Report, p. 7.)

The fact is that Barack Obama supported a proposal to ban gun stores within 5 miles of a school or park, which would eliminate almost every gun store in America. ("Obama and Gun Control," The Volokh Conspiracy, taken from the Chicago Defender, Dec. 13, 1999.[34]

The fact is that Barack Obama voted not to notify gun owners when the State of Illinois did records searches on them. (Illinois Senate, May 5, 2002, SB 1936 Con., vote 26.)

The fact is that Barack Obama voted against a measure to lower the Firearms Owners Identification card age minimum from 21 to 18, a measure designed to assist young people in the military. (Illinois Senate, March 25, 2003, SB 2163, vote 18.)

The fact is that Barack Obama favors a ban on standard capacity magazines. ("Clinton, Edwards, Obama on gun control," Radio Iowa, Sunday, April 22, 2007.)[35]

The fact is that Barack Obama supports mandatory micro-stamping. (Chicago Tribune blogs, "Barack Obama: NIU Shootings call for action," February 15, 2008.[36]

The fact is that Barack Obama supports mandatory waiting periods. (Independent Voters of Illinois/Independent Precinct Organization general candidate questionnaire, Sept. 9, 1996. The responses on this survey were described in "Obama had greater role on liberal survey," Politico, March 31, 2008.[37]

The fact is that Barack Obama supports repeal of the Tiahrt Amendment, which prohibits information on gun traces collected by the BATFE from being used in reckless lawsuits against firearm dealers and manufacturers. (Barack Obama campaign website: "As president, Barack Obama would repeal the Tiahrt Amendment . . ."[38]

---

[34] http://www.volokh.com/posts/1203389334.shtml

[35] http://learfield.typepad.com/radioiowa/2007/04/clinton_edwards.html

[36] http://blogs.trb.com/news/politics/blog/2008/02/barack_obama_comments_on_shoot.html

[37] http://www. politico.com/news/stories/0308/9269.html

[38] http://www.barackobama.com/issues/urbanpolicy/#crime-and-law-enforcement.

The fact is that Barack Obama supports one-gun-a-month handgun purchase restrictions. (Illinois Senate, May 16, 2003, HB 2579, vote 34.)

The fact is that Barack Obama supports a ban on inexpensive handguns. "Obama and Gun Control," The Volokh Conspiracy, taken from the Chicago Defender, Dec. 13, 1999. [39]

The fact is that Barack Obama supports a ban on the resale of police issued firearms, even if the money is going to police departments for replacement equipment. "Obama and Gun Control," The Volokh Conspiracy, taken from the Chicago Defender, Dec. 13, 1999.[40]

The fact is that Barack Obama supports mandatory firearm training requirements for all gun owners and a ban on gun ownership for persons under the age of 21. "Obama and Gun Control," The Volokh Conspiracy, taken from the Chicago Defender, Dec. 13, 1999.[41]

At a fundraiser in 2008, Obama explains why some people are not supportive of his candidacy, saying they "get bitter" and "they cling to guns or religion or antipathy to people who aren't like them or anti-immigrant sentiment or anti-trade sentiment as a way to explain their frustrations."

In The Audacity of Hope, Obama writes that keeping guns out of inner cities is a moral responsibility.

At a 2004 Senate debate, Obama says the failure of Bush to not authorize a renewal of the assault weapons ban is scandalous and that "assault weapons have only one purpose, to kill people." In 2004, he further acts against a bill that protects home invasions.

VII. Civil War

> "No free man shall ever be debarred the use of arms. The strongest reason for the people to retain the right to keep and bear arms is, as a last resort, to protect themselves against tyranny in government" ~ Thomas Jefferson

---

[39] http://www. volokh.com/posts/1203389334.shtml
[40] http://www.volokh.com/posts/1203389334.shtml
[41] http://www.volokh.com/posts/1203389334.shtml (Justin Clark Texas Chl)

There are thirty-six states that give you the right to carry concealed. Some states, even though you have a carry concealed permit, are now taking that right away from you and confiscating your weapon. Louisiana is one of those states, or at least one county in Louisiana is.

Welcome to Shreveport: Your rights are now suspended. According to Cedric Glover, Mayor of Shreveport, Louisiana, his cops "have a power that the President of these United States does not have." Mayor Glover claimed his police officers had the power to take away certain rights. And would you like to guess which rights he had in mind? Just ask Shreveport resident Robert Baillio, who was pulled over for having two pro-gun bumper stickers on the back of his truck — and had his gun confiscated. While the officer who pulled him over says Baillio failed to use his turn signal, the only questions he had for Baillio concerned guns: Whether he had a gun, where the gun was and if he was a member of a pro-gun organization. There were no requests for a driver's license, proof of insurance or vehicle registration — and no discussion of a turn signal. Accordingly, Baillio told the officer the truth, which led the police officer to search his car without permission and confiscate his gun. However, not only does Louisiana law allow residents to drive with loaded weapons in their vehicles, but Mr. Baillio possessed a concealed carry license! What does such behavior demonstrate, other than transparent political profiling — going so far as to use the infamous Department of Homeland Security report on "Americans of a rightwing persuasion" as a how-to guidebook, no less? Mr. Baillio made no secret of his political affiliations — he proudly displayed an American flag and other pro-freedom stickers and decals on his back windshield. In fact, when Baillio asked the officer if everyone he pulls over gets the same treatment, the officer said "No" and pointed to the back of his truck.

Baillio phoned Mayor Glover to complain about this "suspension of rights" only to find that his city's "commander in chief" was elated to hear about the story. According to Glover, Baillio was "served well, protected well, and even got a consideration that maybe [he] should not have gotten." Thankfully, Mr. Baillio recorded a good bit of that phone call. I've reproduced a chunk of the call below:

Baillio: (in the context of being asked about the presence of a gun) Well, I answered that question honestly, and he disarmed me.
Glover: Which would be an appropriate and proper action, sir.

The fact that you gave the correct answer — it simply means that you did what it is you were supposed to have done, and that is to give that weapon to the police officer so he could appropriately place it in a place where it would not be a threat to you, to him or to anyone in the general public. [...]

Glover: My direction to you is that, had you chosen not to properly identify the fact that you had a weapon and directed that officer to where that weapon was located; had you been taken from the vehicle, and the officer, in the interest of his safety, chose to secure you in a safe position, and then looked, found, and determined that you did, in fact, have a weapon... then, sir, you would have faced additional, [inaudible], and more severe criminal sanctions.

Baillio: So what you're saying is: I give up all my rights to keep and bear arms if I'm stopped by the police: Is that correct?

Glover: Sir, you have no right, when you have been pulled over by a police officer for a potential criminal offense [which would be what?!–DB] to stand there with your weapon at your side in your hand [Baillio's weapon was nowhere near his side or his hand, and Glover knew that.–DB] because of your second amendment rights, sir. That does not mean at that point your second amendment right has been taken away; it means at that particular point in time, it has been suspended.

Will Grigg from ProLibertate, an excellent freedom blog, has this to say: According to Glover, a police officer may properly disarm any civilian at any time, and the civilian's duty is to surrender his gun — willingly, readily, cheerfully, without cavil or question.

From Glover's perspective, it is only when firearms are in the hands of people other than the state's uniformed enforcers/ oppressors that they constitute a threat, not only to the public and those in charge of exercising official violence but also to the private gun owner himself.

"I felt sick," Baillio told NAGR. "My uncles didn't die for this country so I could surrender my rights like a wimp. I felt terrible. I was just thinking of all that my family has done for freedom in this nation — including dying — and here they are disarming me at a traffic stop."

I know this kind of harassment occurs frequently all across the country. In fact, the Department of Homeland Security has on many occasions warned law enforcement officials to "look out for" folks like Mr. Baillio who have bumper stickers that promote ideas such as "liberty." There is danger in the Congress, as well. Right now there is active legislation that seeks to label gun owners like you and me as "terrorists." If you are interested in fighting that piece of legislation, please sign your petition to your Congressman and Senators demanding that you not be labeled a "terrorist." (Dudley Brown Executive Director)

Some believe if Obama gets a second term that he will confiscate all of our weapons. What would you do if that happened? What would happen if this was attempted? There are some states where guns are not registered. He required the military to register all of their personal weapons. Some states require that all new weapons are registered and all old weapons are registered. How do you feel about someone knocking on your door, forcing their way into your home and telling you they are going to take any guns and ammunition you have in your home without remuneration to you? What if you expected them to show up? Would you attempt to hide them? Would you fight to keep them? Would you band together with others to fight for your rights?

There are the many that still have their head in the sand that cannot possibly believe it will happen because there are far too many good people out there for it to be attempted. I am not one of them. I still think of what happened to the Jews when Hitler was in power.

Barack Obama now can pull out all of the stops on gun control as he has nothing to lose. He can impose all the restrictions he wants to and nothing can be done about it. Never mind that the administration has no legal authority to do this. Never mind that his orders circumvent Congress, makes an end run around the Constitution, and short-circuits the idea of representative government. It is another example of the arrogance, over-reach, abuse of authority and contempt for the rule of law that has characterized this administration since the beginning.

His re-election means the return of a Justice Department that has slashed prosecution of Federal gun crimes to the lowest levels in more than a decade, and allowed an invasion of violent drug cartel criminals from Mexico into every community in America. It means a White House freed from the control of American voters, and a president free to prosecute his war on the Right to Keep and Bear Arms with impunity.

"A well regulated Militia, being necessary to the security of a free State, the right of the people to keep and bear Arms, shall not be infringed." -Second Amendment.

Whether you own a gun or not, a candidates' views on your rights to own one, if you so choose, should still be of some importance. The history of the Second Amendment was to put in writing an already pre-existing right for an individual to possess a firearm. It was placed into the constitution to protect U.S. citizens from a corrupt government in search of absolute power. The fear was that perhaps down the line, a corrupt state might try to disarm its citizens to impose rule through military force.

The Second Amendment was put into the Constitution to ensure that freedom could not be stripped away, or prohibited. However, it's no secret that liberals have for a long time been very anti-gun ownership. They don't find the need for an individual to provide some measure of their own security. Only makes sense right? Liberals like for everybody to depend on the State, it's how they get a large majority of their votes. They need people to be dependent, it maintains their power. The liberal will tell you to depend on the rich man for your money, depend on the State for your future, and to depend on the U.N. for your security but what about Independence? Independence to the liberal is "selfishness." Barack Obama just happens to be one of the most liberal politicians in Washington. He is no centrist as he would have you believe, especially when it comes to your rights under the 2nd Amendment. (Jake Collett)[42]

In four years will be the tell. Obama has a Mussolini philosophy of "Everything for the State, nothing outside the State, nothing against the State."It is okay when the government does something like spending all of our social security money, or killing someone by direct order of the president, or some government agency, but if you or I did any of these things, we would be put in prison. There is talking of Obama issuing an executive order banning certain guns. He has been in the business of executive orders without a peep from the Republicans or Congress.

Recently the New York Times ran an article "Let's Give Up on The Constitution." They said our Constitution has saddled us with a dysfunctional political system. Of course, it is only dysfunctional to the liberals. It has worked quite well for 200 years for the conservatives. Instead of arguing about what is to be done, we argue about what James Madison might have wanted done 225 years ago. I frankly do not agree with that. I think the writer of the article should spend a day with Congress and then he would know what he was talking about. He would know about all the deals that were being made and all of the pork that was being developed and all of the dishonesty going on and then he would really have a story to write about. He might want to write a story on let's give up on Congress because they are so corrupt. Why is it that Congress cannot just do one thing because it is the right thing to do for this country and not have a deal attached to it; no pork, no deals, no one making any money, no one getting any favors, no one being owed a favor; just one thing because it is just the right thing to do for a change and everyone feels good about themselves. The Democrats and the President would love to get rid of our Constitution. The President said the Constitution gets in the way of his getting done what he needs to do. The Constitution does not restrain us. It handcuffs the government. If we did not have the Constitution, it would free the

---

[42]   http://www.zimbio.com/US+Politics+and+Current+Events/articles/778/
The+2nd+Amendment+to+Obama

government and enslave the people. I hope everyone realizes this. It is protecting the people.[43]

Now with the frenzy from the Sandy Hook Elementary School, Obama vows to put the weight of his office behind gun control and push forward with legislation to remove handguns from The People of this Country, and Senator Dianne Feinstein (D-California) drafted legislation banning firearms, demanding registration and finger-printing. If the Federal government wants to start a new Civil War, all they need to do is go ahead with gun confiscation. Americans are not going to back down or give in. Feinstein's legislation proposes to ban 120 specific weapons.

The proposed restrictions would have absolutely no impact on what happened at Sandy Hook Elementary School. The Legislators are going after the American Public instead of trying to keep what happened at Sandy Hook from happening again. They are going after law-abiding gun owners and targeting owned firearms and ammuni-tion feeding devices. These restrictions will not stop the next mur-der(s) from wreaking just as much havoc and destruction and our government knows this. This is just a ploy to eventually remove all guns from the American public.

Since this tragedy at Sandy Hook, the FBI said they set a record number of background checks in December of 2.8 million over 1.9 million in December of 2011. Should this increase in sales bother the United States Government, the Senate and the House of Representatives? Are they listening to the American People? The FBI has been listening. Many alliances, associations, societies, coalitions, federations and defense leagues have also been listening and group-ing together.

According to Feinstein, lawmakers, and anti-gun zealots, you do not need more than 10 rounds for self-defense. It is always the lib-erals that try to tell the conservatives what they need. Feinstein's leg-islation would ban ammunition magazines that hold more than 10 rounds. Obviously the Second Amendment was specifically created

---

[43] http://politicaloutcast.com/2013/01/constitutional-law-professor-et-rid-of-the-constitution /#ixzz2GlKtndma

and designed to protect "The People" from government bureaucrats like her.

The State of New York passed gun legislation after the Newton tragedy. Politicians said everyone had to register their guns and then they started talking about confiscation. Threats of imprisoning gun owners of up to a year are being issued by the governor's office. God Bless America! The Citizens of New York are saying "we are not going to register our guns. We are not going to do it. They're taking one of our guaranteed civil rights, and they're taking it away."

It is not enough to threaten "The People." The Government has to be able to back it up with force. If Congress passes Feinstein's bill, they are in big trouble with America. Millions of gun owners are going to ignore it. This will be the largest act of civil disobedience that will be seen by the American people as an act of faithfulness and loyalty to our Constitution and our Second Amendment.

Many local government agencies will protect gun owners because they are elected officials and gun owners are voters. Some will not. Sheriff Bruce of Colorado and Richard Mack of Arizona and Sheriff Berry of Georgia say they will protect the Constitutional rights of their citizens to their dying breath. Sheriff Bruce said he is very strong pro-Second Amendment and approximately 50% of the adult citizens of his county have concealed carry permits. Now other Sheriffs throughout the Country are joining in. Before long, hopefully every Sheriff in America will be in force against the Federal government. "If the Federal government wants to start a new Civil War, all they need to do is go ahead with gun confiscation," Mack said. A lot of citizens would stand up for their Second Amendment rights if they were protected by the Sheriffs.

It seems if you protest against Obama's policies you are considered a terrorist in America, but it is okay to burn the American Flag and call it your First Amendment right.

Obama will hold many records before he leaves office. Some he will not be so proud of. Some he has paid much money not to be found and to be destroyed, but unfortunately when you are in public office, you can have no secrets.

He has done a lot of work for gay rights. But there is also a lot written about his own gay relationships before his running for president when he lived in Chicago. So I can see why he runs in that direction. It is too bad this all did not come out while he was an Illinois Senator. The press practically destroyed Bill Clinton for having sex with Monica Lewinsky and was ready to impeach him, but when it came to light that Obama had sex with a man in his past, it was swept under the carpet and it was not newsworthy. MSNBC did not say anything about it. They might call him the first Gay President, but it would be because of his relinquishment to opposition to same-sex marriage. MSNBC host Chris Matthews spoke of Obama and said "I felt this thrill going up my leg," when he heard Obama speak and said he has cried when he heard Obama speak, but he has never reported anything about Obama having sexual relations with another man, nor is he reporter enough to even investigate it.

One in three conservative Republicans and one in five of all Voters believe Obama is a Muslim and consider him to be the First Muslim President. Actually I believe the statistics for Voters is higher than one in five.

Since Obama's re-election, he has been very in-your-face in his speeches and actions. He is very bold. He is pushing Congress. I think he believes he can go a long way before Congress will attempt to impeach him, or before the American public will attempt to call on Congress for impeachment. The truth is I am not a psychiatrist but I can certainly see that what he is doing is not right. He says he reads a lot of Lincoln and talks a lot about Lincoln, but clearly he is nothing like Abraham Lincoln, and cannot be compared to Abraham Lincoln, and America will never compare him to Abraham Lincoln, if that is what he is trying to impress on the minds of America. He can only admire Lincoln for freeing the slaves and for his treatment of the black man. The only thing he has in common is being from Illinois when he was elected President. Far from it; he will never be known as more than a dismal failure at being a President; a perpetual campaigner; a spender of taxpayer money. He will never equal Lincoln in respect. Lincoln loved this Country. Obama wants to tear this Country apart.

One minute he talks about being bipartisan and working together with Congress. That just does not ever happen. He does not have the patience for bipartisanship. He is like a petulant child having a tantrum. When he does not get his way he runs to his office like "I will show you," and writes an executive order. Now the Administration is after Rush Limbaugh and Fox News. They are the only Free Press that we have left in America and Obama thinks they have to be restrained. It will be interesting to see the fight that comes about in the next four years, and there will be a huge fight, because how dare Fox or Limbaugh challenge anything the Administration or the President says or does. Since Obama has been in office, you have never seen any of the other networks challenge anything at all that Obama has said or done. Fox and Limbaugh have been the only ones that have met the test of good journalism, and the Administration hates them.[44]

In an earlier article, People's World, an official publication of the Communist Party USA (CPUSA), declared that "the ability to live free from the fear or threat of gun violence is a fundamental democratic right — one that far supersedes any so-called personal gun rights allegedly contained in the Second Amendment." The article, entitled, "Fight to end gun violence is key to defending democracy," written by People's World labor and politics reporter Rick Nagin, claims that "the right-wing extremists opposing all efforts to curb gun violence are the same forces that rallied behind Republican presidential candidate Mitt Romney, hoping to undermine every other democratic right as well as the living standards of workers and ordinary Americans." "It is for that reason," declares Nagin, "as well as the need to protect public safety, that the same coalition of labor and its allies that worked so hard and effectively to re-elect President Barack Obama must now go all-out to back his common sense proposals for gun law reform." "The Second Amendment is obsolete and now has been twisted to threaten the basic safety and security of all Americans," says Nagin.[45]

---

[44] http://www.breitbart.com/Big-Journalism/2013/01/27/Obama-threatens
[45] http://www.teaparty.org/communists-cheer-on-obamas-gun-grab-19227/

Yet, below is an article from a reporter from Pravda, a Russian Newspaper, that bears repeating.

"This will probably come as a total shock to most of my Western readers, but at one point, Russia was one of the most heavily armed societies on earth. This was, of course, when we were free under the Tsar. Weapons, from swords and spears to pistols, rifles and shotguns were everywhere, common items. People carried them concealed, they carried them holstered. Fighting knives were a prominent part of many traditional attires and those little tubes criss-crossing on the costumes of Cossacks and various Caucasian peoples? Well those are bullet holders for rifles.

'Various armies, such as the Poles, during the Смута (Times of Troubles), or Napoleon, or the Germans even as the Tsarist state collapsed under the weight of WW1 and Wall Street monies, found that holding Russian lands was much, much harder than taking them and taking was no easy walk in the park but a blood bath all its own. In holding, one faced an extremely well-armed and aggressive population Hell bent on exterminating or driving out the aggressor.

'This well-armed population was what allowed the various White factions to rise up, no matter how disorganized politically and militarily they were in 1918 and wage a savage civil war against the Reds. It should be noted that many of these armies were armed peasants, villagers, farmers and merchants, protecting their own. If it had not been for Washington's clandestine support of and for the Reds, history would have gone quite differently.

'Moscow fell, for example, not from a lack of weapons to defend it, but from the lying guile of the Reds. Ten thousand Reds took Moscow and were opposed only by some few hundreds of officer cadets and their instructors. Even then the battle was fierce and losses high. However, in the city alone, at that time, lived over 30,000 military officers (both active and retired), all with their own issued weapons and ammunition, plus tens of thousands of other citizens who were armed. The Soviets promised to leave them all alone if they did not intervene. They did not and for that were asked afterwards to come register themselves and their weapons: where they were promptly shot.

'Of course being savages, murderers and liars does not mean being stupid and the Reds learned from their Civil War experience. One of the first things they did was to disarm the population. From that point, mass repression, mass arrests, mass deportations, mass murder, mass starvation were all a safe game for the powers that were. The worst they had to fear was a pitchfork in the guts or a knife in the back or the occasional hunting rifle. Not much for soldiers.

'To this day, with the Soviet Union now dead 21 years, with a whole generation born and raised to adulthood without the SU, we are still denied our basic and traditional rights to self defense. Why? We are told that everyone would just start shooting each other and crime would be everywhere....but criminals are still armed and still murdering and too often, especially in the far regions, those criminals wear the uniforms of the police. The fact that everyone would start shooting is also laughable when statistics are examined.

'While President Putin pushes through reforms, the local authorities, especially in our vast hinterland, do not feel they need to act like they work for the people. They do as they please, a tyrannical class who knows they have absolutely nothing to fear from a relatively unarmed population. This in turn breeds not respect but absolute contempt and often enough, criminal abuse. 'For those of us fighting for our traditional rights, the US 2nd Amendment is a rare light in an ever darkening room. Governments will use the excuse of trying to protect the people from maniacs and crime, but are in reality, it is the bureaucrats protecting their power and position. In all cases where guns are banned, gun crime continues and often increases. As for maniacs, be it nuts with cars (NYC, Chapel Hill NC), swords (Japan), knives (China) or homemade bombs (everywhere), insane people strike. They throw acid (Pakistan, UK), they throw fire bombs (France), they attack. What is worse, is, that the best way to stop a maniac is not psychology or jail or "talking to them", it is a bullet in the head, that is why they are a maniac, because they are incapable of living in reality or stopping themselves.

'The excuse that people will start shooting each other is also plain and silly. So it is our politicians saying that our society is full of incapable adolescents who can never be trusted? Then, please explain how we can trust them or the police, who themselves grew up and came from the same culture?

'No it is about power and a total power over the people. There is a lot of desire to bad mouth the Tsar, particularly by the Communists, who claim he was a tyrant, and yet under him we were armed and under the progressives disarmed. Do not be fooled by a belief that progressives, leftists hate guns. Oh, no, they do not. What they hate is guns in the hands of those who are not marching in lock step of their ideology. They hate guns in the hands of those who think for themselves and do not obey without question. They hate guns in those whom they have slated for a barrel to the back of the ear.

'So, do not fall for the false promises and do not extinguish the light that is left to allow humanity a measure of self respect."[46]

Take a look at Obama's record over his last term in office. It is not attractive. Then take an honest look at what you can expect in the next four years. I have outlined it here in this book and if you do not believe me, after reading what I am writing below, maybe you will believe me.

He has killer drones flying around the United States and primed to kill United States citizens;

He has jailed United States citizens without due process;

He has installed an Assassination Czar and citizens have been assassinated by the Obama regime;

He has been actively seeking out top military officials willing to fire on U.S. citizens;

He is stockpiling billions of hollow point killer rounds by the alphabet agencies;

Obama's regime is demanding the disarmament of America; Obama is grabbing your guns without rhyme or reason; Obama is destroying the Constitution and targeting the Second Amendment.

The fact is that Barack Obama has endorsed a 500% increase in the Federal excise tax on firearms and ammunition. ("Obama

---

46 http://english.pravda.ru/opinion/columnists/28-12-2012/123335-americans_guns-0/

and Gun Control," The Volokh Conspiracy, taken from the Chicago Defender, Dec. 13, 1999.)[47]

The fact is that Barack Obama has endorsed a complete ban on handgun ownership. (Independent Voters of Illinois/Independent Precinct Organization general candidate questionnaire, Sept. 9, 1996. The responses on this survey were described in "Obama had greater role on liberal survey," Politico, March 31, 2008.[48]

The fact is that Barack Obama supports local gun bans in Chicago, Washington, D.C., and other cities. (David Wright, Ursula Fahy and Sunlen Miller, "Obama: 'Common Sense Regulation' On Gun Owners' Rights," ABC News' "Political Radar" Blog.[49]

The fact is that Barack Obama voted to uphold local gun bans and the criminal prosecution of people who use firearms in self-defense. (Illinois Senate, SB 2165, March 25, 2004, vote 20 and May 25, 2004, vote 3.)

The fact is that Barack Obama supports gun owner licensing and gun registration. ("Fact Check: No News in Obama's Consistent Record." Obama '08, December 11, 2007.[50]

The fact is that Barack Obama refused to sign a friend-of-the-court Brief in support of individual Second Amendment rights in the Heller case.

The fact is that Barack Obama opposes Right to Carry laws. ("Candidates' gun control positions may figure in Pa. vote," Pittsburgh Tribune-Review, Wednesday, April 2, 2008, and "Keyes, Obama Are Far Apart on Guns," Chicago Tribune, 9/15/04.[51]

---

[47]   http://www.volokh.com/ posts/1203389334.shtml
[48]   http://www.politico.com/news/stories/0308/9269.html
[49]   http://blogs.abcnews.com, 2/15/08.
       http://blogs.abcnews.com/politicalradar/2008/02/obama-common-se.html
[50]   http://www.barackobama.com/factcheck/2007/12/11/fact_check_no_news_
       in_obamas_c.php
[51]   http:// www.pittsburghlive.com/x/pittsburghtrib/news/s_560181.html

VIII

Social Security

loyd Blankfein, an enormously wealthy CEO of Goldman Sacs, recently told CBS News that he felt that the retirement age must be changed. He also stated that "maybe some of the benefits have to be affected and maybe some of the inflation adjustments have to be revised. But in general, entitlements have to be slowed down and contained." It is Blankfein's opinion that Social Security wasn't devised to be a system that supported you for a 30-year retirement after a 25-year career. This is from someone that made $16 million in compensation in 2011. My social security is not even pocket change to him. Maybe he would like to donate a year's salary *to the Social Security Fund.*

Maybe they should just pay back the money from the bailout before giving advice that we never asked for.

President Franklin Roosevelt, a democrat, was the one that introduced the Social Security Program (FICA). He said it would be strictly voluntary. Well, that did not last very long before it became mandatory. Participants started paying 1% of the first $1,400 of their annual incomes into the Program. Now it is 7.65% on the first $90,000.

Then the money the participants elected to put into the Program would be deductible from their income tax for tax purposes every year. Now it is no longer tax deductible.

Under Roosevelt, the money the participants put into the independent 'Trust Fund' rather than into the general operating fund, would only be used to fund the Social Security Retirement Program, and no other Government program. When Lyndon Johnson, a democrat, became President, with the democratically controlled house and senate, the money was moved to the general fund and was spent.

They said that the annuity payments to the retirees would never be taxed as income, under Clinton & Gore, up to 85% of your Social Security can be taxed.

And the best of all, Jimmy Carter and the Democratic Party decided to give payments to Immigrants moving into this country, at age 65, even though they never paid a dime into the system.

And now the Democrats tell you that the Republicans want to take your Social Security away and uninformed citizens believe it. The President gets on television and threatens that he cannot guarantee that the senior citizens will receive their social security checks or that the military will receive their checks, or that the veterans will receive their pension checks if the debt ceiling is not raised. This is a threat to all of America in order to get his way in Congress. Now Obama is proposing cutting the healthcare benefits of our veterans – you know, all of those brave men and women that have given so much so that we can have the freedom that he is trying to take away from us. This will not only undermine recruitment into the military, but retention of those already in the military, which is part of the Administration's overall plan in decreasing the present military in preparation of Obama's new militia. It is the soldier, not the President that gives us democracy. It is the soldier, not the Congress, who takes care of us. It is the soldier, not the Reporter, that gives us Freedom of the Press. It is the soldier, not the poet that has given us Freedom of Speech. It is the soldier, not the campus organizer who has given us the freedom to demonstrate. It is the soldier that salutes the flag, who serves beneath the flag, and whose coffin is draped by the flag, which allows the protestor to burn the flag. (Father Dennis O'Brien, U.S. Marine Corp. Chaplain)

I did not hear anything about a reduction in Obama's staff or a reduction in pay for the senators or representatives. As a matter of fact, they just gave themselves another raise – again. I did not hear that the President or the First Lady was going to forego one of their million dollar vacations or just one trip on Air Force One that we pay for daily, or that he was willing to give up a month's pay. Yet Obama has the gall to stand before the nation and threaten not to pay us our own "earned money" which the American people have paid into all of our working lives.

Let us hold the paychecks of all of the House and Senate and even the politicians that have retired and see how fast they resolve all the crises they threaten the nation with. If they would actually do some work instead of making deals to line their own pockets and filling the Bills with Pork once in a while, maybe this country would work a little more economically.

Maybe the IRS could even go after all of the government employees that have not paid income taxes in the last several years. Nearly all of the government employees do not pay income taxes and nobody goes after them. But let one of "The People," not pay Taxes that are owed and the government will put a lien on your home and sell it.

I wish everyone would contact their Senators and Representatives and remind them that they earned their retirement income that the government so generously spends like it was their money to spend and not our money. I wish everyone would contact their Senators and Representatives and remind them that we were the ones that paid and continue paying into Medicare and that we have earned the right to Social Security and Medicare and they do not have the right to spend our Social Security and Medicare money.

I think they need reminding, because they seem to have forgotten that it is our money they are spending and not their money, and now they want to raise taxes to get more money, and for anyone that has an IRA or a 401k, they want that also. Why? Because they have already depleted our Social Security funds and cannot pay it back. Our government is broke. They keep raising the age of retirement and even that is not helping. They are now spending the money that is coming in daily from people that are not yet on social security and that is supposed to be replenishing the Fund and it is not enough. They call that tweaking, but Congress has gone beyond tweaking.

The government refers to our Social Security as a Federal Benefit Payment. It is not a benefit payment. It is earned income. They think if they call it a Federal Benefit Payment that we will forget that it is our money and that we did not earn it.

Not only did we contribute to our social security, but our employer also contributed. It totaled 15% of our income before taxes. If you averaged $30,000 per year over your working life, that is close to $180,000.00 invested in Social Security. If you calculate the future value of your monthly investment in social security ($375.00 a month, including both your and your employer's contributions) at a meager 1% interest rate compounded monthly, after 40 years of working you would have more than $1.3+ million dollars saved! This is your personal investment. Upon retirement, if you took out only 3% per year, you would receive $39,318.00 per year, or $3,277 per month. That is almost three times more than today's average Social Security benefit of $1,230 per month, according to the Social Security Administration. What happens to the money from the people that paid into Social Security who died and never ever got to collect that first check? Many people die between the ages of 55 and 61 and never get to collect Social Security. That is a lot of money that the government keeps – well I should say spends.

Social Security has asked for contractors to supply them with 174,000 rounds of .357 Sig 125 grain bonded jacketed hollow point pistol ammunition. The ammo is to be shipped to 41 locations across the country. The Administration is purchasing the ammo in preparation for civil unrest. Social Security is estimated to keep approximately 40% of senior citizens out of poverty. Should we have an economic collapse, the Federal Reserve has already told banks to prepare for domestic disorder if people are refused their benefits? With the government spending our social security funds, we are closer to this event than you think. What will happen to our senior citizens if the government does not send out their social security checks? What will happen to all future social security recipients that are expecting to retire and have no other source of income? Many retirees have no children that can support them. Many retirees are going into retirement because they are unable to continue in the work force. I put this on the head of everyone that voted for this administration and I hope you can support me because I am unable to hold a job.

IX

Thanksgiving

Thanksgiving under socialism is different this year and next year will be even more different. First we will review Thanksgiving for Thanksgiving past and what we were *Your retirement fund would last more than 33 years (until you're 98 if you retire at age 65)! I can only imagine how much* better most average-income people could live in retirement if our government had invested our money in low-risk interest-earning accounts. Instead, the folks in Washington pulled off a bigger Ponzi scheme than Bernie Madoff ever did. They took our money and used it elsewhere. They want us to "forget" that it was OUR money they were taking. They didn't have a referendum to ask us if we wanted to lend the money to them. They just took it and spent it like it was theirs to spend and each month as more money comes in, they spend that also.

Obama talks about getting jobs for the jobless, but he seems to think there are two kinds of jobs: construction jobs on the highway and building bridges. Of course those would be union jobs, so he would be pushing that kind of work. But he does not seem to know of any other kind of employment. (Unions elect him)

He does not bat an eye at all when he puts people out of work. He just put another coal company down. American Electric Power, or A.E.P., the nation's biggest consumer of coal, announced that it would shut its coal-burning boilers at the Big Sandy electric power plant near Louisa, Ky., a 1,100-megawatt facility that since the early 1960s has been burning coal that was mined locally.

The power company withdrew a plan to spend $1 billion to retrofit Big Sandy so that it could continue to operate. But that would have required a 31 percent increase in electricity rates for eastern Kentucky residents.

Why has this happened? Strict new Government environmental regulations are forcing large utilities to spend billions of dollars to retrofit old coal-burning plants or shut them down, replacing them in most cases with equipment that uses cleaner-burning natural gas.[52]

brought up for Thanksgiving to mean.

In 1789, George Washington issued a Thanksgiving Proclamation as follows:

George Washington's Thanksgiving Proclamation, 1789
***by President George Washington | Washington, DC |
LifeNews.com | 11/22/12 11:21 AM By the President
of the United States of America, a Proclamation.***

Whereas it is the duty of all Nations to acknowledge the providence of Almighty God, to obey his will, to be grateful for his benefits, and humbly to implore his protection and favor – and whereas both Houses of Congress have by their joint Committee requested me to recommend to the People of the United States a day of public thanksgiving and prayer to be observed by acknowledging with grateful hearts the many signal favors of Almighty God especially by affording them an opportunity peaceably to establish a form of government for their safety and happiness.

---

[52] http://conservativebyte.com/2012/12/obama-shuts-down-coal-plant/
#ixzz2FiuIPhW3

Now therefore I do recommend and assign Thursday the 26th day of November next to be devoted by the People of these States to the service of that great and glorious Being, who is the beneficent Author of all the good that was, that is, or that will be – That we may then all unite in rendering unto him our sincere and humble thanks – for his kind care and protection of the People of this Country previous to their becoming a Nation – for the signal and manifold mercies, and the favorable interpositions of his Providence which we experienced in the course and conclusion of the late war – for the great degree of tranquility, union, and plenty, which we have since enjoyed – for the peaceable and rational manner, in which we have been enabled to establish constitutions of government for our safety and happiness, and particularly the national One now lately instituted – for the civil and religious liberty with which we are blessed; and the means we have of acquiring and diffusing useful knowledge; and in general for all the great and various favors which he hath been pleased to confer upon us.

And also that we may then unite in most humbly offering our prayers and supplications to the great Lord and Ruler of Nations and beseech him to pardon our national and other transgressions – to enable us all, whether in public or private stations, to perform our several and relative duties properly and punctually – to render our national government a blessing to all the people, by constantly being a Government of wise, just, and constitutional laws, discreetly and faithfully executed and obeyed to protect and guide all Sovereigns and Nations (especially such as have shewn kindness unto us) and to bless them with good government, peace, and concord – To promote the knowledge and practice of true religion and virtue, and the encrease of science among them and us – and generally to grant unto all Mankind such a degree of temporal prosperity as he alone knows to be best.

Given under my hand at the City of New York the third day of October in the year of our Lord 1789.

President Abraham Lincoln's 1863 Thanksgiving Proclamation by President Abraham Lincoln | Washington, DC | LifeNews. com | 11/22/12 1:11 PM

The year that is drawing toward its close has been filled with the blessings of fruitful fields and healthful skies. To these bounties, which are so constantly enjoyed that we are prone to forget the source from which they come, others have been added which are of so extraordinary a nature that they cannot fail to penetrate and soften even the heart which is habitually insensible to the ever-watchful providence of Almighty God.

In the midst of a civil war of unequaled magnitude and severity, which has sometimes seemed to foreign states to invite and to provoke their aggression, peace has been preserved with all nations, order has been maintained, the laws have been respected and obeyed, and harmony has prevailed everywhere, except in the theater of military conflict, while that theater has been greatly contracted by the advancing armies and navies of the Union.

Needful diversions of wealth and of strength from the fields of peaceful industry to the national defense have not arrested the plow, the shuttle, or the ship; the ax has enlarged the borders of our settlements, and the mines, as well as the iron and coal as of our precious metals, have yielded even more abundantly than heretofore. Population has steadily increased notwithstanding the waste that has been made in the camp, the siege, and the battlefield, and the country, rejoicing in the consciousness of augmented strength and vigor, is permitted to expect continuance of years with large increase of freedom.

No human counsel hath devised nor hath any mortal hand worked out these great things. They are the gracious gifts of the Most High God, who, while dealing with us in anger for our sins, hath nevertheless remembered mercy.

It has seemed to me fit and proper that they should be solemnly, reverently, and gratefully acknowledged, as with one heart and one voice, by the whole American people. I do therefore invite my fellow-citizens in every part of the United States, and also those who are in foreign lands, to set apart and observe the last Thursday of November next as a day of thanksgiving and praise to our beneficent Father who dwelleth in the heavens.

And I recommend to them that while offering up the ascriptions justly due to Him for such singular deliverances and blessings they do also, with humble penitence for our national perverseness and disobedience, commend to His tender care all those who have become widows, orphans, mourners, or sufferers in the lamentable civil strife in which we are unavoidably engaged, and fervently implore the imposition of the Almighty hand to heal the wounds of the nation and to restore it, as soon as may be consistent with the divine purpose, to the full enjoyment of peace, harmony, tranquility, and union.

4th Straight Year: Obama Thanksgiving Resolution Doesn't Thank God by Steven Ertelt | Washington, DC | LifeNews.com | *11/22/12 1:53 PM*

For the fourth straight year, the Thanksgiving resolution from President Barack Obama fails to actually thank God — which is the fundamental reason why Thanksgiving is observed.

In 1789, President George Washington issued a proclamation that set forth the main reason for Thanksgiving, saying, "Now therefore I do recommend and assign Thursday the 26th day of November next to be devoted by the People of these States to the service of that great and glorious Being, who is the beneficent Author of all the good that was, that is, or that will be. That we may then all unite in rendering unto him our sincere and humble thanks – for his kind care and protection of the People of this Country previous to their becoming a Nation."

President Abraham Lincoln, who made Thanksgiving a national holiday, also understood the religious context upon which it was founded.

"It has seemed to me fit and proper that they should be solemnly, reverently, and gratefully acknowledged, as with one heart and one voice, by the whole American people. I do therefore invite my fellow-citizens in every part of the United States, and also those who are in foreign lands, to set apart and observe the last Thursday of November next as a day of thanksgiving and praise to our beneficent Father who dwelleth in the heavens," he wrote.

But, to President Obama, Thanksgiving is about food and football, according to his official remarks as distributed by the White House.

"For us, like so many of you, this is a day full of family and friends; food and football. It's a day to fight the overwhelming urge to take a nap – at least until after dinner," Obama said.

In the third paragraph of the Thanksgiving message, Obama moves on to politics.

"That's especially important this year. As a nation, we've just emerged from a campaign season that was passionate, noisy, and vital to our democracy. But it also required us to make choices – and sometimes those choices led us to focus on what sets us apart instead of what ties us together; on what candidate we support instead of what country we belong to," he said.

Obama eventually mentions blessings and later, in passing, says, "Because there but for the grace of God go I." The rest of the message is a nice one about helping the hurricane victims, honoring our troops, and bringing Americans together. But nowhere in the text is there an actual thanks to the Lord for his blessings on the nation or a recognition that that is the reason for Thanksgiving.

Conservative writer Ben Shapiro noticed this and points out that this is the fourth year in a row in which Obama has not actually thanked God in his Thanksgiving message.

"But, of course, we're used to this. In 2011, there was no mention of God at all. In 2010, Obama was closer, but still missed the mark ("we'll spend some time taking stock of what we're thankful for: the God-given bounty of America, and the blessings of one another"). In 2009, Obama didn't thank God, either."

The modern day Thanksgiving traces its origin to a 1621 celebration at the Plymouth Plantation where the Plymouth settlers held a harvest feast after a successful growing season. This was continued in later years, first as an impromptu religious observance, and later as a civil tradition. Thanksgiving was celebrated by the Pilgrims following their first harvest in 1621. Their feast lasted three days and was attended by 53 Pilgrims and 90 Native Americans. The colonists were accustomed to celebrating with days of prayer and thanking God for blessings for military victories or the end of a drought. However, there were earlier documented thanksgivings in the Commonwealth of Virginia as early as 1607 and with the first permanent settlement at Jamestown, Virginia holding a Thanksgiving in 1610.

Thanksgiving was founded as a religious observance for all the members of the community to give thanks to God for a common purpose. Historic reasons for community thanksgivings are: the 1541 thanksgiving mass after the expedition of Francisco Vásquez de Coronado safely crossing the high plains of Texas and finding game, and the 1777 thanksgiving after the victory in the Revolutionary War Battle of Saratoga. In his 1789 Proclamation, President Washington gave many noble reasons for a national Thanksgiving, including "for the civil and religious liberty", for "useful knowledge", and for God's "kind care" and "His Providence". The only presidents to express a specifically Christian perspective in their proclamation have been Grover Cleveland in 1896, and William McKinley in 1900. Several other presidents have cited the Judeo-Christian tradition. Gerald Ford's 1975 declaration made no clear reference to any divinity, and none of Barack Obama's declarations to date have made more than a passing reference to any divinity.[53]

The tradition of giving thanks to God is continued today in various forms. Various religious and spiritual organizations offer worship services and events on Thanksgiving themes the weekend before, the day of, or the weekend after Thanksgiving.

At home it is a holiday tradition in many families to begin the Thanksgiving dinner by saying Grace either before or after the meal. Some hold their hands in front of them. Others hold hands around the table. Prayer is usually led by the host, but sometime it is led by a special guest, or a designated guest. Sometimes everyone contributes.

Thanksgiving is one of the biggest celebrations of the year and now the liberals are also turning it into something other than a day of giving thanks to God for His blessings. The day after Thanksgiving was given to you as family day so that everyone could have four whole days off from work to enjoy with family. And so, after a quick prayer of thank you for this food and for allowing us to share it with the family today, the girls leave mom in the kitchen to do the dishes and then they are off to the mall and the guys are off to the den to

---

[53] http://en.wikipedia.org/wiki/Thanksgiving_%28United_ States%

watch football. That is, if a prayer was said in your household this past Thanksgiving. Was it, or do you take all of your blessings for granted?

Then commercialism steps in and all of a sudden we have "Black Friday." Before Thanksgiving even arrives, all of the Christmas decorations are put up in the stores and the advertisements and songs are on the radio and television in anticipation of your Christmas shopping on Thanksgiving eve and you are going to the mall the day after Thanksgiving. It is the shopping day of the year that retailers rely on to put them in the black. Now the retailers are opening on Thanksgiving eve and sometimes earlier in the day and this cuts into the employee's family time. It shifts the focus from a day of thanks and celebration of family and friends to a day of shopping. Instead of being a day of thanks, it is becoming black Thursday.

It still comes down to you. If you stay home all day on Thanksgiving with your family, the retailers cannot blackmail you. As long as you go to the mall, the shops will be open. They know all about greed.

X

Abortion

Many of you voted democrat on the issue of what you thought was your female right to choose without actually understanding what that right was. The issue of whether or not the government had a right to force the Catholic Church to pay for birth control pills came up and I believe many of you completely misunderstood the issue altogether. The Catholic Church said we do not have to and the government said yes you do and turned it into an insurance issue and turned it around so that you thought it was something entirely different and that it was a woman's right's issue and not a birth control pill. You sold your soul for a free birth control pill. You did not bother to find out what the issue really was. And confusion was what Obama wanted. It gave him votes.

And for those in Florida that were on a budget, I hope you were watching for specials. Over Black Friday, Planned Parenthood had a special of $10 off for abortions. Can you believe that? $10 off for the murder of your unborn child. Who doesn't want to make things easier for the murder of the unborn. We might as well make it easier on our way to get our nails done or on the way to Starbucks. You will be back to normal in no time.

The Center for Disease Control released new national abortion figures, which the mainstream media ignores, that the number of women dying from legal abortions has doubled. It is the highest since 1994. There is a child murdered by its mother every 94 seconds. This is not by an automatic weapon. This is an abortion by Planned Parenthood.

The Federal government gave Planned Parenthood $542.4 million in "government health services grants and reimbursements." This includes "payments from Medicaid managed care plans."

Below is Obama's actions and records on Born Alive Infant Protection Act:

2001
- Senate Bill 1095, Born Alive Infant Protection Act
- Obama's "no" vote in the IL Senate Judiciary Committee here, March 28, 2001
- Transcript of Obama's verbal opposition to Born Alive on the IL Senate floor, March 30, 2001, pages 84-90
- Obama's "present" vote on the IL Senate floor, March 30, 2001

2002
- *Senate Bill 1662, Born Alive Infant Protection Act*
- Transcript of Obama taking credit for Christ Hospital's Comfort Room in the IL Senate Judiciary Committee hearing, March 5, 2002
- *Obama's "no" vote in the IL Senate Judiciary Committee, March 6, 2002*
- Transcript of Obama's verbal opposition to Born Alive on the IL Senate floor, April 4, 2002, pages 28-35
- *Obama's "no" vote on the IL Senate floor, April 4, 2002*

Listen to audio from Obama's 2002 IL Senate floor debate wherein he argued that while babies might be aborted alive, it would be a "burden" to a mother's "original decision" to assess and treat them.

Meanwhile, the Federal Born Alive Infants Protection Act with a "neutrality clause" added passed the U.S. Senate 98-0, the U.S. House overwhelmingly, and was signed into law August 5, 2002. The pro-abortion group NARAL expressed neutrality on the bill.

2003
- ***Senate Bill 1082, Born Alive Infant Protection Act***
- Democrats took control of the IL Senate with the 2002 elections. This year Born Alive was sent to the Health & Human Services Committee, chaired by Barack Obama.
- As can be seen on the vote docket, Obama first voted to amend SB1082 to add the "neutrality clause" from the federal version of Born Alive to the IL version to make them absolutely identical. (DP#1 means "Do Pass Amendment #1.)
- Then Obama voted against the identical version. (DPA means, "Do Pass as Amended.)
- ***Additional corroboration of Obama's vote: IL State Senate Republican Staff Analysis of SB 1082, March 12-13, 2003, bottom of page 2***

For 4 years following his 2003 vote Obama misrepresented it, stating the wording of the IL version of Born Alive was not the same as the Federal version, and he would have voted for it if so. As recently as August 16, 2008, Obama made this false assertion. But when evidence presented was irrefutable, Obama's campaign on August 18, 2008, admitted the truth to the New York Sun.

The nonpartisan group FactCheck.org has since corroborated Obama voted against identical legislation as passed overwhelmingly on the Federal level and then misrepresented his vote.[54]

Does anyone ever stop and think about whether an unborn child has any rights to live? Certainly it sits in the belly of an emotional mother who most likely is not equipped to make the best decision for it. Mother is making a decision for mother, not for baby. There are places where a pregnant woman can go these days to have a child

---

[54] http://freedomoutpost.com/2013/01/planned-parenthood-aided-the-murder-of-children-at-a-rate-of-1-ever y-94-seconds/#ixzz2JPVkxioi

and there certainly is not the stigma anymore of being an "unwed" mother. Many women choose to be "single" mothers. I personally think a child should have a mother and a father, but if it happens otherwise, I am certainly against abortions.

An unborn child is not worthless. But that presents a problem for the mother's right to choose. If the unborn child is called precious, it compromises mom's right to choose. Is it precious, or is it a disposable human waste product? It is still a viable human becoming that has a right to live and could someday become a great artist, a great singer, a nobody, but nevertheless has a right to life the same as everyone else. Why should this fetus pay for mom's mistake or her being in the wrong place at the wrong time with its life? What about the Sixth Commandment?[55]

I am one of those that believe that life begins at conception. I have watched the tapes that prove it. The scientific evidence is in. I would hope that anyone that spouts off that "I have a right to choose," that you would watch one of those tapes. Because the next time you thought about murdering one of your unborn children, you might change your mind because you would think about that heartbeat you saw on one of those tapes and think that it was your child's heartbeat. I have a dear friend that had an abortion 35 years ago and she regrets it to this day. You will never forget it.

There are approximately 3,700 abortions performed every day. That is killing a living, breathing human becoming. Life is precious. Just think, if your mother aborted you, you would not be living today.

Yes, you do have the right to decide whether or not you want to be pregnant. Yes, you do have the right to decide whether you want to have this child. And you should have thought about that before you were sleeping around and you should have been using contraceptives and being more responsible. Whether it was just a mistake, or whether you were raped, yes, you are the owner of your own body and have the right to decide what to do with it and whether to give birth, but the baby has life from the time the mother's egg is fertilized and that human being should have its own rights. Who is going to be

---

[55] http://www.jillstanek.com/2008/02/links-to-barack-obamas-votes-on-illinois-born-alive-infant-protection-act/

the responsible party and represent it? It should be the mother. And if you believe in God, you will do the right thing. Like it or not, those are the hard facts. I believe abortion is wrong because it ends the life of another human being. Unfortunately, it is legal for a mother to kill her unborn child up to 21 weeks.

However, our Declaration of Independence states that "all men are created equal, that they are endowed by their Creator with certain unalienable Rights, that among these are Life, Liberty and the pursuit of Happiness." Our founding fathers were incredibly particular about the wording used in this document, they didn't just throw it together. They purposefully worded every sentence in the whole Declaration, none of it was random, and so it is with this sentence. "Life, Liberty and the Pursuit of Happiness" were put in that order for a reason, one cannot have liberty or the pursuit of happiness without life. When a woman has an abortion, she is putting her liberty and pursuit of happiness above the life of the child.[56]

Look for this President, who is the most pro-abortionist president ever, to look for new ways to force taxpayers to fund abortions and to promote promiscuity, resulting in countless more abortions. And he thinks it is okay for your child to have an abortion without your consent.

It is not just abortions. The Government is going after your children in schools before they are even teenagers. It is the schools that teach sex education, not the parents. But are the parents teaching the children right from wrong and abstinence? Does the Government have the right to step in and give the children birth control pills and morning after pills free and then say it is so the children can get an education instead of having babies? Is it really not saying to the child that it is okay to go ahead and be promiscuous? Is the school not teaching the child to be immoral instead of teaching the child right from wrong?

---

[56] http://wiki.answers.com/Q/Why_is_abortion_wrong

XI

Religious Freedom

Our government has no problem with your religious freedom as long as it is confined to being practiced within the confines and boundaries of the walls of your church, or your home.

And if it is in your home, make sure that you are not joined by others. And do not let your faith impact your daily life, your work, your decisions, or your activities. They (big brother) do not like that. Our religious freedom is now being removed little by little so that we are not supposed to notice that it is being taken away from us.

This President pushed for repeal of "Don't Ask Don't Tell" to let openly practicing homosexuals serve in our military. (FRC Action)

An article by faith and American freedom historian David Barton has recently been published detailing no less than 50 anti-Christian and anti-Jewish actions of the president since his inauguration in January 2009. Barton's findings have led him to proclaim that President Obama is "America's Most Biblically Hostile U.S. President," which is also the title of his document.

The full list of grievances is broken down into four categories: Acts of hostility toward people of biblical faith, Acts of hostility from the Obama-led military toward people of Biblical faith, Acts of hostility toward biblical values, and Acts of preferentialism for Islam.

Barton said it would not be accurate to simply call him anti-Catholic. Barton shares his reasons for calling Obama anti-biblical:

"Perhaps the most accurate description of his antipathy toward Catholics, Protestants, religious Jews and the Jewish nation would be to characterize him as 'anti-biblical,'…And then when his hostility toward biblical people of faith is contrasted with his preferential treatment of Muslims and Muslim nations, it further strengthens the accuracy of the anti-biblical descriptor. In fact, there have been numerous clearly documented times when his pro-Islam positions have been the cause of his anti-biblical actions."

Acts of hostility toward people of Biblical faith:

- April 2008 – Obama speaks disrespectfully of Christians, saying they "cling to guns or religion" and have an "antipathy to people who aren't like them."
- February 2009 – Obama announces plans to revoke conscience protection for health workers who refuse to participate in medical activities that go against their beliefs, and fully implements the plan in February 2011.
- April 2009 – When speaking at Georgetown University, Obama orders that a monogram symbolizing Jesus' name be covered when he is making his speech.
- May 2009 – Obama declines to host services for the National Prayer Day (a day established by federal law) at the White House.
- April 2009 – In a deliberate act of disrespect, Obama nominated three pro-abortion ambassadors to the Vatican; of course, the pro-life Vatican rejected all three.
- October 19, 2010 – Obama begins deliberately omitting the phrase about "the Creator" when quoting the Declaration of Independence – an omission he has made on no less than seven occasions.

- November 2010 – Obama misquotes the National Motto, saying it is "E pluribus unum" rather than "In God We Trust" as established by federal law.
- January 2011 – After a federal law was passed to transfer a WWI Memorial in the Mojave Desert to private ownership, the U.S. Supreme Court ruled that the cross in the memorial could continue to stand, but the Obama administration refused to allow the land to be transferred as required by law, and refused to allow the cross to be re-erected as ordered by the Court.
- February 2011 – Although he filled posts in the State Department, for more than two years Obama did not fill the post of religious freedom ambassador, an official that works against religious persecution across the world; he filled it only after heavy pressure from the public and from Congress.
- April 2011 – For the first time in American history, Obama urges passage of a non-discrimination law that does not contain hiring protections for religious groups, forcing religious organizations to hire according to federal mandates without regard to the dictates of their own faith, thus eliminating conscience protection in hiring.
- August 2011 – The Obama administration releases its new health care rules that override religious conscience protections for medical workers in the areas of abortion and contraception. November 2011 – Obama opposes inclusion of President Franklin Roosevelt's famous D-Day Prayer in the WWII Memorial.
- November 2011 – Unlike previous presidents, Obama studiously avoids any religious references in his Thanksgiving speech.
- December 2011 – The Obama administration denigrates other countries'religious beliefs as an obstacle to radical homosexual rights.

- January 2012 – The Obama administration argues that the First Amendment provides no protection for churches and synagogues in hiring their pastors and rabbis.
- February 2012 – The Obama administration forgives student loans in exchange for public service, but announces it will no longer forgive student loans if the public service is related to religion.

Acts of hostility from the Obama-led military toward people of Biblical faith:

- June 2011 – The Department of Veterans Affairs forbids references to God and Jesus during burial ceremonies at Houston National Cemetery.
- August 2011 – The Air Force stops teaching the Just War theory to officers in California because the course is taught by chaplains and is based on a philosophy introduced by St. Augustine in the third century AD – a theory long taught by civilized nations across the world (except America).
- September 2011 – Air Force Chief of Staff prohibits commanders from notifying airmen of programs and services available to them from chaplains.
- September 2011 – The Army issues guidelines for Walter Reed Medical Center stipulating that "No religious items (i.e. Bibles, reading materials and/or facts) are allowed to be given away or used during a visit."
- November 2011 – The Air Force Academy rescinds support for Operation Christmas Child, a program to send holiday gifts to impoverished children across the world, because the program is run by a Christian charity.
- November 2011 – The Air Force Academy pays $80,000 to add a Stonehenge-like worship center for pagans, druids, witches and Wiccans.
- February 2012 – The U. S. Military Academy at West Point disinvites three star Army general and decorated war hero Lieutenant General William G. ("Jerry") Boykin

(retired) from speaking at an event because he is an outspoken Christian.

- February 2012 – The Air Force removes "God" from the patch of Rapid Capabilities Office (the word on the patch was in Latin: Dei).
- February 2012 – The Army orders Catholic chaplains not to read a letter to parishioners that their archbishop asked them to read.
- May 2012 – The Obama administration opposes legislation to protect the rights of conscience for military chaplains who do not wish to perform same-sex marriages in violation of their strongly-held religious beliefs.
- June 2012 – Bibles for the American military have been printed in every conflict since the American Revolution, but the Obama Administration revokes the long-standing U. S. policy of allowing military service emblems to be placed on those military Bibles.

Acts of hostility toward Biblical values:

- January 2009 – Obama lifts restrictions on U.S. government funding for groups that provide abortion services or counseling abroad, forcing taxpayers to fund pro-abortion groups that either promote or perform abortions in other nations.
- January 2009 – President Obama's nominee for deputy secretary of state asserts that American taxpayers are required to pay for abortions and that limits on abortion funding are unconstitutional.
- March 2009 – The Obama administration shut out pro-life groups from attending a White House-sponsored health care summit.
- March 2009 – Obama orders taxpayer funding of embryonic stem cell research.
- March 2009 – Obama gave $50 million for the UNFPA, the UN population agency that promotes abortion and

works closely with Chinese population control officials who use forced abortions and involuntary sterilizations.

- May 2009 – The White House budget eliminates all funding for abstinence-only education and replaces it with "comprehensive" sexual education, repeatedly proven to increase teen pregnancies and abortions. 34 He continues the deletion in subsequent budgets.
- May 2009 – Obama officials assemble a terrorism dictionary calling pro-life advocates violent and charging that they use racism in their "criminal" activities.
- July 2009 – The Obama administration illegally extends federal benefits to same-sex partners of Foreign Service and Executive Branch employees, in direction violation of the federal Defense of Marriage Act.
- September 16, 2009 – The Obama administration appoints as EEOC Commissioner Chai Feldblum, who asserts that society should "not tolerate" any "private beliefs," including religious beliefs, if they may negatively affect homosexual "equality."
- July 2010 – The Obama administration uses federal funds in violation of federal law to get Kenya to change its constitution to include abortion.
- August 2010 – The Obama administration Cuts funding for 176 abstinence education programs.
- September 2010 – The Obama administration tells researchers to ignore a judge's decision striking down federal funding for embryonic stem cell research.
- February 2011 – Obama directs the Justice Department to stop defending the federal Defense of Marriage Act.
- March 2011 – The Obama administration refuses to investigate videos showing Planned Parenthood helping alleged sex traffickers get abortions for victimized underage girls.
- July 2011 – Obama allows homosexuals to serve openly in the military, reversing a policy originally instituted by George Washington in March 1778.

- September 2011 – The Pentagon directs that military chaplains may perform same-sex marriages at military facilities in violation of the federal Defense of Marriage Act.
- October 2011 – The Obama administration eliminates federal grants to the U.S. Conference of Catholic Bishops for their extensive programs that aid victims of human trafficking because the Catholic Church is anti-abortion.

Acts of preferentialism for Islam:

- May 2009 – While Obama does not host any National Day of Prayer event at the White House, he does host White House Iftar dinners in honor of Ramadan.
- April 2010 – Christian leader Franklin Graham is disinvited from the Pentagon's National Day of Prayer Event because of complaints from the Muslim community.
- April 2010 – The Obama administration requires rewriting of government documents and a change in administration vocabulary to remove terms that are deemed offensive to Muslims, including jihad, jihadists, terrorists, radical Islamic, etc.
- August 2010 – Obama speaks with great praise of Islam and condescendingly of Christianity.
- August 2010 – Obama went to great lengths to speak out on multiple occasions on behalf of building an Islamic mosque at Ground Zero, while at the same time he was silent about a Christian church being denied permission to rebuild at that location.
- 2010 – While every White House traditionally issues hundreds of official proclamations and statements on numerous occasions, this White House avoids traditional Biblical holidays and events but regularly recognizes major Muslim holidays, as evidenced by its 2010 statements on Ramadan, Eid-ul-Fitr, Hajj, and Eid-ul-Adha.
- October 2011 – Obama's Muslim advisers block Middle Eastern Christians' access to the White House.

- February 2012 – The Obama administration makes effulgent apologies for Korans being burned by the U. S. military, 54 but when Bibles were burned by the military, numerous reasons were offered why it was the right thing to do.

Many of these actions are literally unprecedented – this is the first time they have happened in four centuries of American history. The hostility of President Obama toward Biblical faith and values is without equal from any previous American president.

Endnotes

1. Sarah Pulliam Baily, "Obama: 'They cling to guns or religion'," Christianity Today, April 13, 2008. (Return)
2. Aliza Marcus, "Obama to Lift 'Conscience' Rule for Health Workers," Bloomberg, February 27, 2009; Sarah Pulliam Baily, "Obama Admin. Changes Bush 'Conscience' Rule for Health Workers," Christianity Today, February 18, 2011. (Return)
3. Jim Lovino, "Jesus Missing From Obama's Georgetown Speech," NBC Washington, April 17, 2009. (Return)
4. Johanna Neuman, "Obama end Bush-era National Prayer Day Service at White House," Los Angeles Times, May 7, 2009. (Return)
5. Chris McGreal, "Vatican vetoes Barack Obama's nominees for U.S. Ambassador," The Guardian, April 14, 2009. (Return)
6. Meredith Jessup, "Obama Continues to Omit 'Creator' From Declaration of Independence," The Blaze, October 19, 2010. (Return)
7. "Remarks by the President at the University of Indonesia in Jakarta, Indonesia," The White House, November 10, 2010. (Return)
8. LadyImpactOhio, "Feds sued by Veterans to allow stolen Mojave Desert Cross to be rebuilt," Red State, January 14, 2011. (Return)

9. Marrianne Medlin, "Amid criticism, President Obama moves to fill vacant religious ambassador post," Catholic News Agency, February 9, 2011; Thomas F. Farr, "Undefender of the Faith," Foreign Policy, April 5, 2012. (Return)

10. Chris Johnson, "ENDA passage effort renewed with Senate introduction," Washington Blade, April 15, 2011. (Return)

11. Chuck Donovan, "HHS's New Health Guidelines Trample on Conscience," Heritage Foundation, August 2, 2011. (Return)

12. Todd Starns, "Obama Administration Opposes FDR Prayer at WWII Memorial," Fox News, November 4, 2011. (Return)

13. Joel Siegel, "Obama Omits God From Thanksgiving Speech, Riles Critics," ABC News, November 25, 2011. (Return)

14. Hillary Rodham Clinton, "Remarks in Recognition of International Human Rights Day," U.S. Department of State, December 6, 2011. (Return)

15. Ted Olson, "Church Wins Firing Case at Supreme Court," Christianity Today, January 11, 2012. (Return)

16. Audrey Hudson, "Obama administration religious service for student loan forgiveness," Human Events, February 15, 2012. (Return)

17. "Houston Veterans Claim Censorship of Prayers, Including Ban of 'God' and 'Jesus'," Fox News, June 29, 2011. (Return)

18. Jason Ukman, "Air Force suspends ethics course that used Bible passages that train missle launch officers," Washington Post, August 2, 2011. (Return)

19. "Maintaining Government Neutrality Regarding Religion," Department of the Air Force, September 1, 2011. (Return)

20. "Wounded, Ill, and Injured Partners in Care Guidelines," Department of the Navy (accessed on February 29, 2012). (Return)

21. Air Force Academy Backs Away from Christmas Charity," Fox News Radio, November 4, 2011. (Return)

22. Jenny Dean, "Air Force Academy adapts to pagans, druids, witches and Wiccans," Los Angeles Times, November 26, 2011. (Return)

23. Ken Blackwell, "Gen. Boykin Blocked At West Point," cnsnews.com, February 1, 2012. (Return)

24. Geoff Herbert, "Air Force unit removes 'God' from logo; lawmakers warn of 'dangerous precedent'," syracuse.com, February 9, 2012. (Return)

25. Todd Starnes, "Army Silences Catholic Chaplains," Fox News Radio, February 6, 2012. (Return)

26. Markeshia Ricks, "Bible checklist for Air Force lodges going away," Air Force Times, April 16, 2012. (Return)

27. Patrick Goodenough, "White House 'Strongly Objects' to Legislation Protecting Military Chaplains from Doing Same-Sex Weddings or Being Forced to Act Against Conscience," cnsnews.com, May 16, 2012. (Return)

28. "U.S. military insignia no longer allowed on Bibles," CBN News, June 14, 2012. (Return)

29. Jeff Mason and Deborah Charles, "Obama lifts restrictions on abortion funding," Reuters, January 23, 2009. (Return)

30. "Obama pick: Taxpayers must fund abortions," World Net Daily, January 27, 2009. (Return)

31. Steven Ertelt, "Pro-Life Groups Left Off Obama's Health Care Summit List, Abortion Advocates OK," LifeNews, March 5, 2009. (Return)

32. "Obama Signs Order Lifting Restrictions on Stem Cell Research Funding," Fox News, March 9, 2009. (Return)

33. Steven Ertelt, "Obama Administration Announces $50 Million for Pro-Forced Abortion UNFPA," LifeNews, March 26, 2009; Steven Ertelt, "President Barack Obama's Pro-Abortion Record: A Pro-Life Compilation," LifeNews, February 11, 2012. (Return)

34. Steven Ertelt,"Barack Obama's Federal Budget Eliminates Funding for Abstinence-Only Education," LifeNews, May 8, 2009. (Return)

35. Steven Ertelt, "Obama Budget Funds Sex Ed Over Abstinence on 16-1 Margin," LifeNews, February 14, 2011. (Return)

36. Steven Ertelt, "Obama Admin Terrorism Dictionary Calls Pro-Life Advocates Violent, Racist," LifeNews, May 5, 2009. (Return)

37. "Memorandum for the Heads of Executive Departments and Agencies,"The White House, June 17, 2009. (Return)

38. Matt Cover, "Obama's EEOC Nominee: Society Should 'Not Tolerate Private Beliefs' That 'Adversely Affect' Homosexuals," cnsnews.com, January 18, 2010. (Return)

39. Tess Civantos, "White House Spent $23M of Taxpayer Money to Back Kenyan Constitution That Legalizes Abortion, GOP Reps Say," Fox News, July 22, 2010. (Return)

40. Steven Ertelt, "Obama, Congress Cut Funding for 176 Abstinence Programs Despite New Study," LifeNews, August 26, 2010. (Return)

41. Steven Ertelt, "President Barack Obama's Pro-Abortion Record: A Pro-Life Compilation," LifeNews, February 11, 2012. (Return)

42. Brian Montopoli, "Obama administration will no longer defend DOMA," CBSNews, February 23, 2011. (Return)

43. Steven Ertelt, "Obama Admin Ignores Planned Parenthood Sex Trafficking Videos," LifeNews, March 2, 2011. (Return)

44. Elisabeth Bumiller, "Obama Ends 'Don't Ask, Don't Tell' Policy," New York Times, July 22, 2011; George Washington, The Writings of George Washington, John

45. Fitzpatrick, editor (Washington: U. S. Government Printing Office, 1934), Vol. XI, pp. 83-84, from General Orders at Valley Forge on March 14, 1778. (Return)

46. Luis Martinez, "Will Same Sex Marriages Pose a Dilemma for Military Chaplains?," ABC News, October 12, 2011. (Return)

47. Jerry Markon, "Health, abortion issues split Obama administration and Catholic groups," Washington Post, October 31, 2011. (Return)
48. Barack Obama, "Remarks by the President at Iftar Dinner," The White House, September 1, 2009; Kristi Keck, "Obama tones down National Day of Prayer observance," CNN, May 6, 2009; Dan Gilgoff, "The White House on National Day of Prayer: A Proclamation, but No Formal Ceremony," U.S. News, May 1, 2009. (Return)
49. "Franklin Graham Regrets Army's Decision to Rescind Invite to Pentagon Prayer Service," Fox News, April 22, 2010. (Return)
50. "Obama Bans Islam,Jihad From National Security Strategy Document," Fox News, April 7, 2010; "Counterterror Adviser Defends Jihad as 'Legitimate Tenet of Islam'," Fox News, May 27, 2010; "'Islamic Radicalism' Nixed From Obama Document," CBSNews, April 7, 2010. (Return)
51. Chuck Norris, "President Obama: Muslim Missionary? (Part 2)," Townhall.com, August 24, 2010; Chuck Norris, "President Obama: Muslim Missionary?," Townhall.com, August 17, 2010.(Return)
52. Barack Obama, "Remarks by the President at Iftar Dinner," The White House, August 13, 2010; "Obama Comes Out in Favor of Allowing Mosque Near Ground Zero," Fox News, August 13, 2010; Pamela Geller, "Islamic Supremacism Trumps Christianity at Ground Zero," American Thinker, July 21, 2011. (Return)
53. "WH Fails to Release Easter Proclamation," Fox Nation, April 25, 2011; "President Obama ignores most holy Christian holiday; AFA calls act intentional," American Family Association (accessed on February 29, 2012). (Return)
54. "Report: Obama's Muslim Advisers Block Middle Eastern Christians' Access to the White House," Big Peace (accessed on February 29, 2012). (Return)

55. Masoud Popalzai and Nick Paton Walsh, "Obama apologizes to Afghanistan for Quran burning," CNN, February 23, 2012. (Return)
56. "Military burns unsolicited Bibles sent to Afghanistan," CNN, May 22, 2009. (Return)[57]

You should not be surprised when religion is pushed out of the work place through the Employment Non-Discrimination Act. In some cases, it may have been done so already. If the President can get this enacted, it would force people to check their moral convictions at the door of their home even if they owned their own business.

When the schools took religion and God out of the schools, they did just the opposite. They promoted immorality and unrestrained philandering. They allow the girls to come to school in mini dresses and the boys to come to school with their pants down to their knees. They call it the in-thing, but it looks more like a quickie.

This President has abandoned the Defense of Marriage Act (DOMA)—and his constitutional oath to enforce the law of the land—coming out strongly in support of same-sex "marriage." The Bible in Leviticus 20:13 (New American Standard Bible) states: "If there is a man who lies with a male as those who lie with a woman, both of them have committed a detestable act; they shall surely be put to death. Their bloodguiltiness is upon them." And perhaps a better understanding is found at Romans 1:25-32 (New American Standard Bible) which states: "For they exchanged the truth of God for a lie, and worshiped and served the creature rather than the Creator, who is blessed forever. Amen. For this reason God gave them over to degrading passions; for their women exchanged the natural function for that which is unnatural. And in the same way also the men abandoned the natural function of the woman and burned in their desire towards one another, men with men committing indecent acts and receiving in their own persons the due penalty of their error. And just as they did not see fit to acknowledge God any longer, God gave them over to a depraved mind, to do those things which are not proper, being filled with all unrighteousness,

---

[57]   http://www.wallbuilders.com/LIBissuesArticles.asp?id=106938

wickedness, greed, malice, full of envy, murder, strife, deceit, malice, they are gossips, slanderers, haters of God, insolent, arrogant, boastful, inventors of evil, disobedient of parents, without understanding, untrustworthy, unloving, unmerciful; and although they know the ordinance of God, that those who practice such things are worthy of death, they not only do the same, but also give hearty approval to those who practice them."

Not only does this Administration promote homosexualty, it causes the Board of Education to force the local schools to promote homosexualty. This Administration is intent on weakening the family as a unit and is keeping the pressure on.

Through the secular-"progressive"looking-glass,the term"sexual orientation" has, in a few short years, evolved to accommodate an ever-expanding fruit basket of carnal appetites. First it was lesbians, gays and bisexuals. Then they added transgenders.

Because it is illegal to discriminate based on gender identity, and since we are now "required" to be "tolerant," the transgender can legally fully expose themselves to the opposite sex and to try to do anything about it is considered a hate crime.

They have not added "bestiality" to the program as yet, although it is in the making. Frank Kameny is saying that sex with animals is okay as long as the animal doesn't mind, and the animal rarely does.

A man in Florida accused of sexual activity with a miniature donkey filed a motion asking a judge to declare the Florida statute banning sexual activities with animals unconstitutional.

Once our culture decides, as a matter of course, that all morality is relative,all bets are off.Once we determine,as a matter of law,that people are entitled to special privilege because they subjectively define their identity based upon deviant sexual proclivities and behaviors, moral, legal and cultural anarchy are inevitable.[58]

Barack Obama compares himself to Abraham Lincoln. Yet he does everything opposite of Lincoln. Abraham Lincoln would rise out of his grave and ride on the White House if he knew what Obama was intending to do in this next four years to this country.

---

[58]　http://politicaloutcast.com/2013/01/a-politically-incorrect-guide-to-sexual-orientation/#ixzz2GlHzc0le

Our schools systems have been threatened by atheists for so long that the school boards automatically believe the Bible and everything Christian should be banned from the public schools. In reality atheists are bullies trying to force their views on schools and the public when many of those views violate the constitutional rights of the students and the people. If it was not for the American Center for Law and Justice working with the students and families in educating the principals on what is and is not violating the separation of church and state, the principals would be violating the students' First Amendment rights all the time as quite often teachers refuse to allow students the right to use biblical references in their homework.

When will Christians stand up for their rights and stand up to the atheists who forcibly trample on the constitutional rights. Why do we let the teachers and the school board ban the Bible or anything Christian from the schools and the education of our children?

While our schools ban Christianity from the school system, the curriculum has a section on Islam where it teaches students a variety of verses from the Quran. "Who Is Allah?" "Allah is the Almighty God." "Allah alone is the Creator. He alone deserves our devout love and worship." The section on Islam also lists verses that malign other religions and then provides instructions on how to convert to Islam.

However, there is nothing about Judaism or Christianity being taught. Do you know what your children are being taught? What is really wrong with this Country? Since the devil tempted Eve and she ate the apple, we have had good and bad. God said do not eat the apple. But the serpent came along and said nothing will happen and so Eve ate the apple. We all have good and bad in us. Then Cain killed Abel. We do not know why. We do not know what kind of weapon was used. We just know that from the beginning of time there was good and bad in human nature. Evil prowls constantly in the world and we must pray for help for us and for our children.

And it is always human nature to point fingers when something goes wrong. And who points the fingers? The anti-gun liberals. They do not point fingers if someone gets killed with a knife. They do not point fingers if someone gets run down by a car. They do not point fingers if 300 people get killed in an airplane crash. But let one person hold up a convenience store and let the owner of the store kill the robber and every anti-gun zealot wants to ban all guns in the United States.

Darrell Scott, the father of Rachel Scott, spoke before the House Judiciary Committee's Subcommittee with regard to Columbine and said the following:

> "Your laws ignore our deepest needs, Your words are empty air. You've stripped away our heritage, You've outlawed simple prayer. Now gunshots fill our classrooms, And precious children die. You seek for answers everywhere, And ask the question "Why?" You regulate restrictive laws, Through legislative creed. And yet you fail to understand, That God is what we need!"

"Men and women are three-part beings. We all consist of body, mind, and spirit. When we refuse to acknowledge a third part of our make-up, we create a void that allows evil, prejudice, and hatred to rush in and wreak havoc. Spiritual presences were present within our educational systems for most of our nation's history. Many of our major colleges began as theological seminaries. This is a historical fact. What has happened to us as a nation? We have refused to honor God, and in so doing, we open the doors to hatred and violence. And when something as terrible as Columbine's tragedy occurs — politicians immediately look for a scapegoat such as the NRA. They immediately seek to pass more restrictive laws that contribute to erode away our personal and private liberties. We do not need more restrictive laws. Eric and Dylan would not have been stopped by metal detectors. No amount of gun laws can stop someone who spends months planning this type of massacre. The real villain lies within our own hearts.

"As my son Craig lay under that table in the school library and saw his two friends murdered before his very eyes, he did not hesitate to pray in school. I defy any law or politician to deny him that right! I challenge every young person in America, and around the world, to realize that on April 20, 1999, at Columbine High School prayer was brought back to our schools. Do not let the many prayers offered by those students be in vain. Dare to move into the new millennium with a sacred disregard for legislation that violates your God-given right to communicate with Him. To those of you who would point your finger at the NRA — I give to you a sincere challenge.. Dare to examine your own heart before casting the first stone!

> "My daughter's death will not be in vain! The young people of this country will not allow that to happen!"
> —Darrell Scott

XII

Our Economy

D
o you not just love our Congress? We elect them to look out for the best interests of our country and they do nothing. And our President! Where is the budget he is supposed to present to Congress in good faith? And the media is not any help either. They keep talking about our going over the fiscal cliff instead of telling us the truth and discussing the real problems.

The fundamentals that drive our fiscal policy will not change regardless of whether a budget deal is struck. We are already heading toward another trillion in debt – an unsustainable burden that will cripple our economy, destroy our currency, and slash our paper investments. No last-minute budget compromise is going to stop that.

On December 31, 2012, the terms of the Budget Control Act of 2012 will go into effect, which means more taxes will go into effect, as well as spending cuts that were agreed upon as part of the debt ceiling farce of 2011. This is necessary in order to add $1.5 Trillion per year for the next six years to our already massive and unsustainable debt.

House Speaker John Boehner has the power to stop this borrowing-and-spending frenzy with one vote of his united caucus. But he has no intentions of doing so. Instead there will be more of the same "o."

Every poll shows overwhelming majorities of Republicans, independents and even Democrats opposed raising the debt limit. But Washington just is not listening.

The politicians will eventually come to some sort of agreement, but it will not help our country. The Feds will keep printing money to try to stave off deflation in favor of inflation. That will probably cause the dollar and paper-based investments to drop. Remember in 2008 when the value of automobiles, stocks, and homes dropped 30%. Remember the United States lost its AAA rating for the first time.

Gold went from $1,500 to $1,925 in just 10 weeks. Because gold does not care about inflation or deflation, it attaches itself to other variables. It has become the best protector against our present and future economy. It offers a possible huge upside since the Fed has started another round of money printing.

Just ask Russia what they think about the American economy. When Vladimir Putin says the United States is endangering the world-wide economy, he is acting on the situation. He just purchased 570 metric tons of gold in the past 10 years. That is more than China according to the IMF data compiled by Bloomberg. When politicians fail, confidence in this country and its leadership drops. I am one of those citizens that has lost confidence in Washington politicians. I have listened to Senators and Representatives carefully over the past four years and I have corresponded with a few of them. They are not seriously interested in any meaningful debt reduction. The Democrats think the government is not spending or borrowing enough.

If you expect anything to change for the better in the next four years, think again. It will not. Obama loves to spend money – our money – and has no intentions of stopping. Inflation will continue on food, gasoline, and heating your home. Get it in your head! The Federal Government does not care anything about whether you have enough money to have a savings account, your ability to put food on the table, or to heat your home. The Government cares about keeping rates low in order to continue servicing the interest on $16.5 trillion of debt, because there is simply no way to pay it back.

Higher taxes for the rich will not slow our economy. Frankly, I cannot imagine being so rich that I do not mind paying higher taxes.

Our Country was built on a free society where each one of us has had a chance to make our own way in life and make our own individual fortunes and for someone to come along and say that you have to share your wealth goes against my grain. I am one of the poor ones and it still goes against my grain. That is unAmerican. If I was rich I would certainly be generous to God, the unfortunate, and charities, but for the Government to step in and tell you that you must pay more in taxes and pay more than your share is totally Marxist – oh, sorry, "progressive" they want you to call it. The government did not tell anyone about the 2.3% Medical Excise Tax that began on January 1st that is hidden from the consumer.

If it is true, as a senior staff reporter of WND stated, that Obama is pushing a plan for private retail stores such as Wal-Mart to create a "new wage floor" that hikes workers' wages by at least 27 percent to $12.25 per hour, this could devastate businesses in some cities. There are 15 million people in the private retail sectors like Wal-Mart, Target, Kroger, Home Depot, Walgreens, Lowe's, Best Buy, Safeway and Macy's. The study was done by a group known as DEMOS, a longtime partner of the disgraced ACORN activist group. They were instrumental in Obama hiring Van Jones, the former White House "green jobs" adviser who resigned after it was exposed he founded a communist revolutionary organization and called for "resistance" against the U.S. government. Jones is now a Demos scholar. The study surmises the pay increase would cost consumers "just cents more per shopping trip on average."

The "living wage" is found in the ideology of Karl Marx, author of the 1848 "Communist Manifesto." "Marx believed that only under communism could he find support for his ultimate goal of a living wage, 'From each according to his ability, to each according to his needs.'"

A "living wage" was implemented in 80 cities from the mid-1990s to 2003, sometimes organized by ACORN. It got its start in the mid-90's in Baltimore when a combination of left-leaning church leaders, unionists and community activists mostly led by ACORN began to push for a "social compact" that included a hike in the minimum wage to $6.10 – 43 percent above the Federal minimum wage at the time – for service workers in hotels and other businesses in the city's redeveloped Inner Harbor, a prime tourist area. But Baltimore's economy soon crashed, with 58,000 jobs disappearing, even as the rest of Maryland added 120,000 jobs and other cities across the country prospered.

Another location that enacted a living wage bill was Milwaukee County, Wisconsin, which passed a law increasing the minimum wage only for city-contracted janitors and security guards to $6.25 an hour. That law was urged on by ACORN and the socialist New Party, which was also instrumental in lobby efforts in Baltimore. The living wage campaign was a main platform of the socialist New Party. That also failed.

If Obama is so right in his theory of recovery, how does he explain the absence of any kind of recovery in four years. I just heard on the news that there was something like an increase in jobs this month of something like 150,000. But they did not say most of them came about because of the clean-up from Hurricane Sandy and that the jobs are temporary.

Obama blamed everything on Bush during his first term. When G.W. Bush was in office, Obama was a Senator (D-Illinois) and opposed raising the debt limit. When he ran for the presidency in 2008 he pledged to reduce the deficit by half in his first term. Instead, he increased borrowing more than all of the other presidents in the history of our Country. Who will he blame during his second term? Now Obama says, "that the best way to generate jobs and growth is for the government to spend more, not less."

Somehow Obama has to be convinced that his policies are wrong. It is the only way we can turn America around. But I do not think that is going to happen.

You may be surprised to learn that schools in the State of Texas for one are teaching that the Second Amendment only applies to state run militias and not private citizens. In other words, they are teaching that there is no constitutional right for Americans to bear or own firearms unless they are part of state operated militia like the National Guard. Never mind you that the United States Supreme Court has ruled in several cases that the Second Amendment does apply to every American citizen.

June 28, 2012 is the day that America officially became a socialist nation. It was a day that marked the end of freedom as we know it. The United States Supreme Court gave the Federal Government unlimited power over our individual lives when it upheld ObamaCare in a 5-4 ruling. As a result, the quality of our healthcare and the freedom to choose our doctors was stripped as was many more of our freedoms. In the future, you will get less health care and there will be fewer doctors.

I have always maintained that Obama was out to destroy our economy. As you listen to the news about the fiscal cliff negotiations, you cannot help but be convinced that Obama is still out to destroy our economy and throw this country into bedlam. Once this happens, he has everything in place where he can declare martial law and seize total and absolute control of the nation, effectively killing free America and establishing a new socialistic and Islamic America.

Everything Obama has done in his first four year term has been detrimental to our economy. ObamaCare has nearly bankrupted us. Now he is driving us over the fiscal cliff, along with Congress.

We have a Congress that can do nothing without adding tons of pork. That is why they cannot come to any agreements.

Look at all of the entitlement packages that Obama has formed to create more poor and to keep them poor.

Republicans and Democrats can continue playing their charade they call "negotiations," but no amount of pretend bickering will prevent ObamaCare's new tax increases from happening. Over the next 10 years, Americans will be subjected to $1 trillion in new taxes. Americans for Tax Reform summarized the top five taxes to be implemented on New Year's Day.

The Medical Device Tax will levy a 2.3% excise tax on gross sales of medical device manufacturers regardless of profit amount. So, they might not profit at all, but their sales will still be taxed at 2.3%. This will contribute even more to the rising cost of healthcare.

The Flex Account Tax will be imposed on the "30-35 million Americans who use a pre-tax Flexible Spending Account (FSA) at work to pay for their family's basic medical needs." FSA accounts will face a new government cap of $2,500, which will end up costing those with FSA's over $13 billion over the next 10 years.

The Investment Income Surtax is a tax on something that's already taxed, a double tax. Currently, capital gains and dividends are taxed at 15%, but with the New Year will come an increase of the capital gains tax to 20% and an increase of the dividends tax to 39.6%. On top of those new tax rates, a 3.8% surtax will be added bringing the capital gains rate to 23.8% and the dividends rate to 43.4%. Those couples making at least $250,000 and those individuals making at least $200,000 will be subjected to the new taxes.

The "Haircut" for Itemized Medical Deductions raises the medical expenses threshold from 7.5% to 10% of one's adjusted gross income (AGI) in order to qualify for a tax deduction. According to ATR, "By limiting this deduction, ObamaCare widens the net of taxable income for the sickest Americans. This tax provision will harm near retirees and those with modest incomes but high medical bills."

The Medicare Payroll Tax increases the rate from 2.9% to 3.8% on all wages and self-employment profits of all those rich people who make more than $200,000 ($250,000 for rich married couples). Employers will continue to pay 1.45%, but employees will experience an increase to 2.35% if they exceed the threshold. Increases in taxes will only further drive prices and healthcare costs up and bankrupt small businesses. These taxes will do nothing to help the economy, except for the economy of politicians who benefit by taking more and more money from hard-working Americans in order to buy votes from other people.[59]

Congress and Obama are playing games as far as the Sequester. Obama has stopped the White House tours, putting people out of work that run the tours. Many wealthy people have believe the tours are important and have come forth and have volunteered to pay for the tours. But, of course, that is not really Obama's purpose in stopping the tours. He is playing games. On March 5, Texas Rep. Louis Gohmert filed an amendment to a House resolution that would prohibit federal funds from being spent on Obama's golf trips until public tours of the White House resumed. So the games are backfiring.

---

[59] http://godfatherpolitics.com/8762/obamacare-brings-in-1-trillion-in-new-taxes-starting-new-years-day/#ixzz2GluJrFxM

XIII

Liberals And Democrats

If you do not know if you are a Republican or a Democrat or if you are a liberal, just take the "fence" test below.

Which side of the fence are you on?

- If a Republican doesn't like guns, he doesn't buy one.
- If a Democrat doesn't like guns, he wants all guns outlawed. If a Republican is a vegetarian, he doesn't eat meat.
- If a Democrat is a vegetarian, he wants all meat products banned for everyone.
- If a Republican is homosexual, he quietly leads his life.
- If a Democrat is homosexual, he demands legislated respect.
- If a Republican is down-and-out, he thinks about how to better his situation.
- If a Democrat is down-and-out he wonders who is going to take care of him.
- If a Republican doesn't like a talk show host, he switches channels.
- If a Democrat doesn't like a show host, A Democrat demands that the program he doesn't like be shut down.
- If a Republican is a non-believer, he doesn't go to church.

- A Democrat non-believer wants any mention of God and religion silenced.
- If a Republican decides he needs health care, he goes about shopping for it, or may choose a job that provides it.
- If a Democrat decides he needs health care, he demands that the rest of us pay for his.
- And so is the difference between Republicans, Democrats, Conservatives and Liberals.
- Is it true that the Ft Hood Shooter, a Muslim, was a Registered Democrat?
- Is it true that the Columbine shooters came from families that were registered Democrats and progressive liberals?
- Was the Virginia Tech Shooter and his parents Registered Democrats?
- Was the Colorado Theater Shooter a staff worker on the Obama campaign, an Occupy Wall Street participant, a progressive liberal, and a Registered Democrat?
- Is it true that the Connecticut School Shooter and his mother were registered Democrats?
- Is it true that the shooter of Congresswoman Gabby Gifford is a registered Democrat?

What is my point you ask? My point is that it is not the Republicans, nor the Independents that are causing all of the problems and screaming for reform. Whenever there is tolerance involved it is on the right. Whenever someone is trying to cram a new law down your throat, you can bet your bippy it is a liberal democrat.

It has been proven that gun legislation does not work, yet the democrats in our government want to enact more gun legislation. It seems that no amount of discussions, no amount of statistical data, can convince them that more legislation will not work because they have it in their head that all guns must be confiscated. They refuse to look at history and the statistics of other countries. They refuse to look at our own Constitution. These are the same Congressman that walked out on the first day that Congress was in Session and Congress went around the room and each Congressman read a paragraph of the Constitution. Remember how many of the Congressmen left the hall because they said our Constitution was archaic? I was so ashamed and wished that America could have fired those that left the room. They deserved to be fired because, after all, they are employees of the American people.

Right now in Washington, D.C., Obama and Biden are doing everything in their power to see that our Second Amendment rights are removed from the Constitution. Although there are others testifying in favor of the Second Amendment, Obama is not listening. He has always been against guns. Of course, he has exceptions. He is not against the guns that protect him now and for the rest of his life, and he is not against the guns that protect his wife and children now and for the rest of their lives. He did just sign a new law making sure it will be for the rest of their lives and not just for ten years as it has always been for past presidents.

Many countries are watching to see what is happening in America and our Constitution. Our freedom has long been admired and now all of a sudden it is being taken from us. Our government is no longer respected and everyone is watching to see what The People will do about it and how long we will put up with it.

I think right now it is a matter of whether there are more Liberals than good old fashioned conservatives. If the conservatives-remain passive, the Liberals will win. But I think the Liberals better watch out, because the good people of this country will rise up and take this country back. The People of this Country are just about sick of the Liberals and being pushed around and they sure are not going to give up their guns.

The time for the Liberals to shine is over. The Conservatives have seen what the Liberals have had to offer and we do not like what is on the menu. Perhaps if their presentation would have been different they would have had different results, but I believe the passive Conservatives are starting to wake up.

A liberal is proud to be called a liberal because they believe they are progressive, broadminded, open-minded and unprejudiced. And that describes a liberal pretty well. It also describes a man of amoral character with no religious values.

XIV

Our Military And Islam

We have a new military manual out now on how to speak to the Afghans. It warns our American Soldiers to avoid talking about certain topics such as pedophilia, which is a part of the Islamic culture. "By mentioning pedophilia and women's rights and saying that soldiers should not mention such things they are tacitly admitting that those things are indeed part of Islam," said Robert Spencer, founder of Jihad Watch.[60]

The manual says attacks against the military may have been brought on by themselves because of their insensitivity towards Islamic Culture, ignorance, or lack of empathy. That is like saying we are not being considerate enough.

Then again, I wonder what they think when they see a couple of our soldiers making out on a hillside. That must curl their toes, or maybe not.

The plain truth is that the Obama Administration has been entertaining convicted terrorists and gays and lesbians in the White House since he has been President. He has Muslim Brotherhood

---

[60] http://www.wnd.com/2012/12/army-acknowledges-pedophilia-part-of-is-lam/#WgJ50s3VG6Ddjvkv.99

members within the State Department purging training materials of anything critical of Islam. How did we get to this point and when will America wake up, rise and take this Country back? All the man has to do is look you in the eye, smile and tell you another lie and you all get that thrill up your leg, is that it? It is Sodom and Gomorrah all over again.

The gay community is celebrating because the United States Supreme Court gave them permission to go to hell and they will have someone to blame when they have to face their maker. Do you think that excuse will get them through the Pearly Gates? And what about the Supreme Court Justices. Will the assenting voters have to answer before God for their sanction of DOMA? Of course, the ACLU is behind this business.

But, in his Opinion, Justice Kennedy wrote, "The federal statute is invalid, for no legitimate purpose overcomes the purpose and effect to disparage and to injure those whom the State, by its marriage laws, sought to protect in personhood and dignity,..." "By seeking to displace this protection and treating those persons as living in marriages less respected than others,the federal statute is in violation of the Fifth Amendment." Justice Kennedy delivered the court's opinion, and was joined by Justices Ruth Bader Ginsburg, Stephen Breyer, Sonia Sotomayor and Elena Kagan. Chief Justice John Roberts and Justices Antonin Scalia and Samuel Alito all filed dissenting opinions. Justice Clarence Thomas joined Scalia's dissent in whole and parts of Alito's opinion.

DOMA was signed by President Bill Clinton in 1996 and prevented same-sex couples whose marriages were recognized by their home state from receiving hundreds of benefits available to other married couples under Federal law. During the Obama administration, the Justice Department initially defended DOMA in court despite the administration's desire to repeal it. But in 2011 the Justice Department decided that the law was unconstitutional and declining to defend it any longer.

The truth is we all must consider the judgment of our higher power, not the judgment of the United States Supreme Court; particularly in these trying times. There are many that considered this a landmark victory. There are many that were saddened by the Verdict. Perhaps had I read the briefs submitted I would be more swayed and understanding, but it still comes down to your eternal soul and are you willing to give that up?

There are still several states that do not have DOMA laws which will now change their position. I am sorry about that. They will do it in the name of progress. There is that word "progressive" again. It is like saying "go to hell" is it not? There are 30 states that have DOMA laws. The court left it to the states to continue in their traditional role of defining lawful marriage – even if Congress cannot – just as churches and other religious institutions have the freedom to decide the spiritual and moral outlines marriage.

States that prefer to sanction marriages that are only between a man and a women may now find it difficult to prevent state judges from using the court's arguments about equality. But the ruling, written by Justice Anthony Kennedy, relies heavily on his long-held concerns about protecting personal liberty.

In a previous decision, Justice Kennedy wrote that "[a] the heart of liberty is the right to define one's own concept of existence, of meaning, of the universe, and of the mystery of human life." He said sex is only a part of "a personal bond that is more enduring." As many well-seasoned married couples know, an enduring marriage relies more on a blending of individual qualities than on sex. As the DOMA ruling stated, marriage comes with responsibilities as much as rights. The state's role is to help spouses live up to the responsibilities they accept in making a life-long commitment. Christian Science Monitor

After the ruling, The Obama administration said it would move swiftly to ensure same-sex married couples get the same tax and other benefits as heterosexual couples, although the process for doing so is uncertain for same-sex couples who marry in one state, then move to a state that doesn't recognize gay marriage.

I say it is a tragic day for traditional marriage. Marriage is the union between one man and one woman. It always has been and always will be. Marriage is the only institution that brings together a man and a woman for life, and provides any child who comes from their union with the secure foundation of a mother and a father.

There is a difference between a man and a woman and a mother and a father. In the Bible, Matthew 19, Jesus refers to male and female and says that man shall leave his mother and father and shall cleave to his wife. I guess it is easier not to believe at all.

The United States Supreme Court's failure to redefine marriage for all states is a major setback for those seeking to redefine natural marriage. Time is not on the side of those seeking to create same-sex 'marriage.'

Given the situation in Egypt and the instability in the North African nations, why is the U.S. sending more than 200 tanks and 20 F-16 aircraft to Egypt from Fort Worth. Sources say it is part of an order that was placed two years ago? Given our fiscal problems, should we be Egypt's major arm's supplier; particularly to Morsi's Muslim Brotherhood?

Did you see what one top Obama supporter is doing to avoid paying a bunch of those new taxes? Jim Sinegal, the co-founder, director and former CEO of Costco, was so smitten by the job Obama is doing that he agreed to give a prime-time address at last year's Democratic convention. So you'd think he'd be hunky-dory with the Obama tax increases, wouldn't you?

Not on your life. Costco announced that it would pay a special dividend to all of its shareholders. It did it — and even borrowing the $3 billion it will cost — so shareholders won't have to pay the higher tax on dividend income. Since Sinegal owns 2 million shares of Costco stock, that's $14 million he'll get in this special dividend. At the current tax rate of 15 percent on dividends, he'll have to fork over a little more than $2 million of it to Uncle Sam. But had Costco waited until January to pay the dividend, Sinegal's tax rate would be 43.4 percent, or more than $6 million. In other words, the former Costco CEO gets to pocket an extra $4 million that otherwise would have gone to the Internal Revenue Service. Merry Christmas! Bob Livingston eletter@news.personalliberty.com. And Costco carries Halal foods.

Drones are no longer just used in Afghanistan. Wrap your head around seeing a drone in American air space and spying on you now. They have military names such as Wasp, Raven and ScanEagle, but these are among hundreds of drones registered to fly over domestic airspace. Governors talk about allowing the State Police to use drones. Some police departments have used drones to enforce traffic laws or to spy on criminal suspects. Is the administration getting prepared for labeling those that don't want to give up their Second Amendment rights as "terrorists?" Will drones start hunting down American citizens under the false label of being a terrorist? According to the Federal Aviation Administration, 348 camera-equipped drones have been approved for domestic use in our American air space, so get ready to be spied on by our own government.

The point is, free Americans are supposed to be left alone. It is prisoners that are supposed to be enclosed and watched all the time. Does this not become a Fourth Amendment issue? What happens if the government decides to change their policy? They certainly are not going to let us know when or if they do. Drones are capable of spying on essentially all Americans all the time. A drone is capable of spying on one American from 15,000 feet in the air. You will not even know you are being spied upon. Actually, it is not the drone, it is the spy equipment and its use that is the real issue, no matter what it is mounted on.

I can see the government gradually letting us get used to the idea of having them around and I can see the left, as usual, being tolerant and thinking it is a good idea – security they will say. The truth is, it is another government infringement on our freedom and we are under a police state and unspoken martial law. For you that think Senator Lindsey Graham is the good guy, think again. He is for the drones flying around.

Sen. Lindsey Graham (R-S.C.) will offer a resolution commending President Barack Obama's use of drones and the killing of Anwar al-Awlaki. "Every member of Congress needs to get on board," Graham said. "It's not fair to the president to let him, leave him out there alone quite frankly. He's getting hit from libertarians and the left. "I think the middle of America understands why you would want a drone program to go after a person like Anwar al-Awlaki," Graham added.

And now the United States are selling drones to Arabia so they can spy on Iran – spy on who?

A good comparison of an armed country to the United States would be Switzerland. Gun ownership is widespread and at least one out of every three inhabitants own a gun. After the U.S., Yemen and Switzerland ranks third on the list of the most guns per person. If an enemy were to invade Switzerland, the people would have to own weapons in order to defend it because they do not have an army. In spite of this, their homicide and suicide rates are low and crime rates in the two countries differ greatly.

The Swiss believe it is because their childhood is relatively free of violence and their children grow up having received significant tolerance and trust. They point to the level of violence in American television and video games that American children are exposed to at a very young age in comparison. It used to be the same in this country. Our parents grew up with everyone owning a gun and our children grew up having received significant tolerance and trust. We did not have television and video games.

Now what do the governments do with all of the assault weapons they have? Well, Canada, for one, the day before this business in Newtown, Ct, opened the door for gun merchants in Canada to sell fully automatic weapons with high-capacity magazines – banned in Canada – to Columbia. This will be under "very strict controls," of course, which include fully automatic firearms, electric stun guns and large-capacity magazines.

It is Russia that is telling Americans to keep their guns. When the Communists took power, they took away all weapons from the Russians. That included all swords and spears to pistols, rifles and shotguns. Communism is only a step up from socialism. People carried them concealed and as traditional attire. When the Communists took power, the first thing they did was disarm the population. Does this sound familiar? From that point, mass repression, mass arrests, mass deportations, mass murder, and mass starvation were all a safe game for the powers.

The Soviet Union has been dead 21 years and they are still denied the right to defend themselves. They are told everyone would start shooting each other, but criminals are still armed and most of those criminals are wearing police uniforms. The Russians like our Second Amendment and are championing us and our right to fight for it.

We often wonder about the dirty dealings of our Government, but are not often privy to reading about them. One of the best that I came across was an article about the Department of Homeland Security awarding a contract of $45,000 to provide them with 200,000 more rounds of bullets. This new purchase adds to the staggering amount of 1.6 million rounds of ammo already purchased by the DHS over the previous 9 months. The bullets were for a basic and advanced training program in South Carolina which specializes in maritime law enforcement and port security.

What is interesting is the contract was awarded to the "Evian Group," an organization formed five days before the contract was let. It seems to be a front and does not have any assets, no address, no website, or phone number. If you google "Evian Group," you can come up with a "think tank" that deals in "globalization — must be for everyone or it will be for no-one".

The contradiction is the Obama administration preaching gun control on the one hand and on the other hand the Federal government arming itself with an arsenal that would be enough to wage a full scale long-term ground war. A citizen is considered to be a prepper-terrorist if he has 1,000 rounds of ammunition. The government can stockpile billions of rounds and the media does not question it. Instead the media uses the double standard and turns on the citizen.

The Federal Government is preparing for a mass civil unrest. In August of 2012, the Department of Homeland Security purchased an additional 750,000 rounds of ammunition to add to its 450,000 rounds of hollow points already purchased in 2012. The Department of Homeland Security also put in an order for riot gear and a number of checkpoint booths with stop and go lights. The United States Army is also buying similar equipment. A recently leaked US Army Military Police training manual for "Civil Disturbance Operations" outlines how military assets are to be used domestically to suppress riots, confiscate firearms and even kill Americans on U.S. soil during mass civil unrest.

The increasing likelihood of a full blown financial collapse in the coming months has also spurred Federal agencies and the U.S. Army to enhance their preparations for domestic chaos on a scale greater than riots witnessed in Europe over the past two years.

In all my years I have often heard the expression "what will they think of next"? And someone always thinks up something that just blows your mind – usually a liberal. And, of course, in the last few years, you do not have to go very far. It is always the main stream media, Congress, or our President.

The President has never liked our military and has always undermined its traditional integrity. He forced the military to accept homosexuality and took action against anyone that opposed that determination.

He attacked the retirement system, making a career less attractive. He took action against Chaplains who stood up for their faith. The Pentagon issued orders for troops in the Middle East to remove all religious symbolism, however this was largely enforced against Christians and Jews, but not for Muslim.

The Obama Administration was outraged when American Soldiers burned a stack of Qurans, but said nothing about the Qurans being defaced by Muslim prisoners and Obama said nothing about the stack of Bibles that were burned at the same time.

Obama has been tailoring the military to his specifications. Many career personnel, including commanding officers began retiring or resigning their commissions, leaving the military to the liberals.

I have always said, and the writer above seems to agree, that it is Obama's intention to destroy America's economy so that he can create a national emergency and declare martial law and establish his own national police force. It is a move towards a Marxist dictatorship. He has 4 years to accomplish this. The only thing to stop him from achieving his goal is our United States Military and he is now weeding out the military by asking each member if they would fire on a fellow American citizen if called upon? He must also somehow disband Congress. We are not alone. Congressman Broun from Georgia also believes that Obama has the same agenda.

On 29 April 2010, at a rally in Quincy, Illinois, a group of "elderly" ladies quietly protested Obama's appearance. They wore t-shirts and hats which suggested they were Tea Party Patriots. Obama called out the swat team and said "We cannot continue to rely on our military in order to achieve the national security objectives we've set. We've got to have a civilian national security force that's just as powerful, just as strong, just as well-funded."

Obama wants a civilian police force to match the size of our military force. He does not trust the military force. At one time he planned on using the Marshall's Service. Then he said he planned on expanding AmeriCorp, a program originally started by Clinton, and a sister to The Peace Corp. AmeriCorp presently has 80,000 members. Each member typically completes 1,700 hours of service over 11 months; these members additionally receive a living allowance, health benefits, and child care assistance during their term. AmeriCorps State and National members engage in direct service activities, such as after-school tutoring or homebuilding, and capacity-building activities, such as volunteer recruitment, for the organizations they serve. After successfully completing their term of service, AmeriCorps State and National members may receive an Education Award of up to $5,550. The Education Award can pay for additional college or graduate school courses, or it can pay off existing student loans.

Successes for individual AmeriCorps members include increasing their commitment to community service, increasing community-based activism, connection to their communities, knowledge of community problems, engagement in the political process, and voting participation. Each member takes the following oath:

> I will get things done for America–to make our people safer, smarter, and healthier.
>
> I will bring Americans together to strengthen our communities. Faced with apathy, I will take action.
>
> Faced with conflict, I will seek common ground. Faced with adversity, I will persevere.
>
> I will carry this commitment with me this year and beyond. I am an AmeriCorps member, and I will get things done.

Whether or not AmeriCorps will want to have Obama as their leader instead of their present leader, and whether AmeriCorps members will want to change their lifestyle and allegiance and start packing guns and swear to fire upon an American citizen if Obama thinks it is necessary is another story. America has been supporting them a long time. They are used to joining AmeriCorp to get an education and performing public service. Their Oath will have to change, because when faced with conflict they will no longer be seeking a common ground of good. If Obama turns AmeriCorp into his national police force, it certainly will no longer meet any of the needs of the communities that it now serves.

Can you imagine someone wanting to take an organization like AmeriCorp that tutors and mentors disadvantaged youths, fight illiteracy, improve health services, builds affordable housing, teaches computer skills, cleans parks and streams, manages or operate after-school programs, helps communities respond to disasters, and build organizational capacity and change all of that into a national police force – just because he wants his own private police force?

Well, not to worry. We have always said that while you are watching Obama's left hand, you must also be watching his right hand. While you were listening to all of his rhetoric about AmeriCorp, he was really busy building his real personal army at the Department of Homeland Security. Fooled me! But that is what he was doing.

It is very obvious that the Department of Homeland Security is filling that role in the Obama regime. The Department of Homeland Security and the Immigration and Customs Enforcement have purchased over 450 million rounds of .40 caliber hollow point ammunitions.

Why is it that the immigration services and enforcement budgets at Homeland Security were nearly $20 billion in 2010? Yet the Mexican-U.S. border was guarded by a "virtual fence" which allowed a continuous flow of illegal aliens over the border. Some 4-5.5 million foreigners have overstayed their Visas in the US, yet just 8,100 arrests have been made by the Homeland Security. In October of 2012, Barack Obama signed an Executive Order creating the "White House Homeland Security Partnership Council," its ostensible purpose to "...advance the federal government's use of local partnerships to address homeland-security challenges." But the DHS was ALREADY working with local governments across the nation.

Obama "he [wanted] to be able to dictate who gets to participate in these local partnerships – and they don't have to be local law enforcement or local government officials to do so. These partnerships will be with 'the private sector, nongovernmental organizations, foundations and community-based organizations.' All of whom will be handpicked by Obama and those federal bureaucrats he appoints."

The National Defense Authorization Act empowers Obama on his own to determine who represents a threat to the United States and to have that individual detained and imprisoned. And the Executive Order he signed allows the president to select like-thinking "deputies" nationwide, authorized to act on Obama's behalf. These men will have little or no concern for the security of the United States. Rather, they will be working exclusively to increase the power of the president by threatening and intimidating his political enemies.

Barack Obama is at last building his Civilian National Security Force. It consists of a thoroughly corrupt organization of the far left, employed by the DHS and empowered by the president himself to ignore the Constitution and the laws of the United States. Representing the 3rd largest department in the federal government, these DHS forces of a Constitutionally ineligible president are working to implement a police state—a dictatorship in which all "rights" will derive from the sole authority of Barack Obama.

You say you do not believe it! Take a look at the facts. Obama has already filled the ranks of our regular military force with gays and lesbians who will follow him to any end because he is their defender. He has tailored the top leaders by asking if they are willing to shoot Americans. Those that answer yes, are put in key positions while those that answer no are basically seeing the end of their military careers. Christianity or Bibles are no longer allowed.

The Department of Homeland Security has been stockpiling millions of weapons and billions of rounds of ammunition. They even have The National Oceanic and Atmospheric Administration stockpiling weapons and ammunition. This has no purpose other than to be used against the American people.

The massive push for gun control has only one purpose and that is to disarm the American people. There are more guns in private ownership than there are people in the US. That would make a hostile takeover more difficult, costly and time consuming. However, the stockpiles of weapons and ammunition are just for that purpose, because Obama knows that there are a lot of Americans who will not give up their guns so easily.[61] Do a little studying of history in nations like Germany, Russia, China and other socialist nations. They all thought it could never happen to them and it did and it all started with a tyrant just like Obama gaining power and outlawing guns!

Make no mistake—Barack Obama has every intention of imposing his will on the American public by creating a Marxist dictatorship during his second term. It is for that reason the assault has begun on American gun owners, as an armed public can fight back and defeat such would-be tyrants.

General James Mattis, head of the United States Central Command,"is being told to vacate his office several months earlier than planned." As reporter Paul Joseph Watson commented: "Concerns over US troops being given orders to fire on American citizens in the event of mass gun confiscation first arose in 1995 when hundreds of Marines at 29 Palms, California were given a survey as part of an academic project by Navy Lieutenant Commander Ernest Guy Cunningham which asked the Marines if they would, 'Fire upon U.S. citizens who refuse or resist confiscation of firearms banned by the United States government.' The survey was subsequently leaked because many of the Marines who took it were shocked by the tone of the question. In July 2012, the process by which this could take place was made clear in a leaked US Army Military Police training manual for 'Civil Disturbance Operations' (PDF) dating from 2006. Similar plans were also outlined in an updated manual released in 2010 entitled FM 3-39.40 Internment and Resettlement Operations. On page 20 of the manual, rules regarding the use of 'deadly force'

---

[61] http://godfatherpolitics.com/9782/obama-poised-for-hostile-military-take-over-of-us/#ixzz2 NAR4RXHQ

in confronting "dissidents" on American soil are made disturbingly clear with the directive that a, 'Warning shot will not be fired.' Given that second amendment advocates are now being depicted as dangerous terrorists by the federal government and local law enforcement, Jim Garrow of Conservative Action Alert's claim is sure to stoke controversy given that Americans are seeing their gun rights eviscerated while the federal government itself stockpiles billions of bullets."

Defense Secretary Gates says now that we are leaving Afghanistan that we no longer need the Marines. We probably will not be downsizing the Navy, but we no longer need the Marine Corp. Gates said he's recognized "an anxiety" about the future of the service, particularly "the perception being that they have become too heavy, too removed" from their roots. But he noted that while the historic image of Marines remains etched in massive beach landings, in reality and in law the service is tasked to carry out "such other duties as the president may direct." Here comes the Militia.

The military retirement system is unsustainable and in dire need of repair, according to an influential Pentagon advisory board. According to Fox News, the Pentagon proposed replacing the military's pension system with a 401(k)-style contribution program. Under the Defense Business Board plan, all troops would receive yearly retirement contributions if they served at least 20 years — a stipulation of the existing system. The money, however, would not vest until service reached at least three to five years and would then be payable at retirement age. If personnel left before that three-to five-year mark, the time served would be rolled over into Social Security. The Pentagon made the proposal as it searches for $400 billion in cuts. But critics of the plan say it will hurt military recruiting as the best candidates will be less likely to launch a military career. Defense Secretary Leon Panetta has said that if the retirement benefits are changed, "you have to do it in a way that doesn't break faith with the military." He also said that the Pentagon would have to grandfather in current benefits.

XV

Our Flag

Does anyone know the history of our flag or even know what the meaning of the flag draped coffin is?

Those who think that America is an arrogant nation should really reconsider that thought. Our founding fathers used God's word and teachings to establish our Great Nation and I think it's time Americans get reeducated about this Nation's history.

Do you know that at military funerals, the 21-gun salute stands for the sum of the numbers in the year 1776?

Have you ever noticed the honor guard pays meticulous attention to correctly folding the United States of America Flag 13 times? You probably thought it was to symbolize the original 13 colonies, but that is not the reason.

The 1st fold of the flag is a symbol of life.

The 2nd fold is a symbol of the belief in eternal life.

The 3rd fold is made in honor and remembrance of the veterans departing the ranks who gave a portion of their lives for the defense of the country to attain peace throughout the world. The 4th fold represents the weaker nature, for as American citizens trusting in God, it is to Him we turn in times ofpeace as well as in time of war for His divine guidance.

The 5th fold is a tribute to the country, for in the words of Stephen Decatur, 'Our Country, in dealing with other countries, may she always be right; but it is still our country, right or wrong.'

The 6th fold is for where people's hearts lie. It is with their heart that they pledge allegiance to the flag of the United States of America, and to the Republic for which it stands, one Nation, under God, indivisible, with Liberty and Justice for all.

The 7th fold is a tribute to its Armed Forces, for it is through the Armed Forces that they protect their country and their flag against all her enemies, whether they be found within or without the boundaries of their republic.

The 8th fold is a tribute to the one who entered into the valley of the shadow of death, that we might see the light of day.

The 9th fold is a tribute to womanhood, and Mothers. For it has been through their faith, their love, loyalty and devotion that the character of the men and women who have made this country great has been molded.

The 10th fold is a tribute to the father, for he, too, has given his sons and daughters for the defense of their country since they were first born.

The 11th fold represents the lower portion of the seal of King David and King Solomon and glorifies in the Hebrews eyes, the God of Abraham, Isaac and Jacob.

The 12th fold represents an emblem of eternity and glorifies, in the Christians eyes, God the Father, the Son and Holy Spirit. The 13th fold, or when the flag is completely folded, the stars are uppermost reminding them of their Nations motto, 'In God We Trust.'

After the flag is completely folded and tucked in, it takes on the appearance of a cocked hat, ever reminding us of the soldiers who served under General George Washington, and the Sailors and Marines who served under Captain John Paul Jones, who were followed by their comrades and shipmates in the Armed Forces of the United States, preserving for them the rights, privileges and freedoms they enjoy today.

There are some traditions and ways of doing things that have deep meaning.

In the future, you'll see flags folded and now you will know why.

The national flag of the United States of America, often simply referred to as the American flag, consists of thirteen equal horizontal stripes of red (top and bottom) alternating with white, with a blue rectangle in the canton (referred to specifically as the "union") bearing fifty small, white, five-pointed stars arranged in nine offset horizontal rows of six stars (top and bottom) alternating with rows of five stars. The 50 stars on the flag represent the 50 states of the United States of America and the 13 stripes represent the thirteen British colonies that declared independence from the Kingdom of Great Britain and became the first states in the Union. Nicknames for the flag include the "Stars and Stripes", "Old Glory", and "The Star-Spangled Banner."

Desecration of the American Flag is considered an outrage by the American People, but remains protected as Freedom of Speech. Chapter 1 of Title 4 of the United States Code (4 U.S.C. § 1 et seq). is a U.S. Federal law, a flag code, but there is no penalty for failure to comply with it. In fact, the U.S. Supreme Court has ruled that punitive enforcement would conflict with the First Amendment right to freedom of speech. Now, that is too bad.

Standards of respect

The flag should never be dipped to any person or thing, unless it is the ensign responding to a salute from a ship of a foreign nation. This is sometimes misreported as a tradition that comes from the 1908 Summer Olympics in London, where countries were asked to dip their flag to King Edward VII: American team flag bearer Ralph Rose did not follow this protocol, and teammate Martin Sheridan is often, though apocryphally, quoted as proclaiming that "this flag dips before no earthly king." This tradition was codified as early as the 1911 U.S. Army drill regulations.

The flag should never be displayed with the union (the starred blue union) down, except as a signal of dire distress in instances of extreme danger to life or property.

The flag should not be used as "wearing apparel, bedding, or drapery", or for covering a speaker's desk, draping a platform, or for any decoration in general (exception for coffins). Bunting of blue, white and red stripes is available for these purposes. The blue stripe of the bunting should be on the top.

The flag should never be drawn back or bunched up in any way. The flag should never be used as a covering for a ceiling.

The flag should never be used for any advertising purpose. It should not be embroidered, printed, or otherwise impressed on such articles as cushions, handkerchiefs, napkins, boxes, or anything intended to be discarded after temporary use. Advertising signs should not be attached to the staff or halyard. The flag should never be fastened, displayed, used, or stored in such a manner as to permit it to be easily torn, soiled, or damaged in any way.

The flag should not be used as part of a costume or athletic uniform, except that a flag patch may be used on the uniform of military personnel, firefighters, police officers, and members of patriotic organizations.

Flag lapel pins may also be worn (they are considered replicas) and are worn near the heart.

The flag should never have placed on it, or attached to it, any mark, insignia, letter, word, number, figure, or drawing of any kind.

The flag should never be used as a receptacle for receiving, **_holding, carrying, or delivering anything. The flag should never be stepped on._**

In a parade, the flag should not be draped over the hood, top, sides, or back of a vehicle, railroad train, or boat. When the flag is displayed on a motorcar, the staff shall be fixed firmly to the chassis or clamped to the right fender.

When the flag is lowered, no part of it should touch the ground or any other object; it should be received by waiting hands and arms. To store the flag it should be folded neatly and ceremoniously.

The flag should be cleaned and mended when necessary.

If the flag is being used at a public or private estate, it should not be hung (unless at half-staff or when an all-weather flag is displayed) during rain or violent weather.

When a flag is so tattered that it can no longer serve as a symbol of the United States, it should be destroyed in a dignified manner, preferably by burning. The American Legion, Boy Scouts of America, Girl Scouts of the USA, National Sojourners, and other organizations regularly conduct dignified flag-burning ceremonies, often on Flag Day, June 14.

The flag should never touch anything beneath it. Contrary to an urban legend, the flag code does not state that a flag that touches the ground should be burned. Instead, it is considered disrespectful to the flag and the flag in question should be moved in such a manner so it is not touching the ground.

The flag should always be permitted to fall freely. (An understandable exception was made during the Apollo moon landings when the flag hung from an extensible horizontal bar, allowing full display even in the absence of an atmosphere.)

Displaying the flag outdoors

When the flag is displayed from a staff projecting from a window, balcony, or a building, the union should be at the peak of the staff unless the flag is at half-staff. When it is displayed from the same flagpole with another flag, the flag of the United States must always be at the top except that the church pennant may be flown above the flag during church services for Navy personnel when conducted by a Naval chaplain on a ship at sea.

When the flag is displayed over a street, it should be hung vertically, with the union to the north or east. If the street runs north-south, the stars should face east. For streets running east-west, the stars should face north. If the flag is suspended over a sidewalk, the flag's union should be farthest from the building and the stars facing away from it.

When the United States flag is displayed with the flags of states of the union or municipalities, and not with the flags of other nations, the federal flag, which represents all states, should be flown above and at the center of the other flags. 4 U.S.C. § 7(e). The other flags may be the same size but none may be larger.

No other flag should be placed above it. The flag of the United States is always the first flag raised and the last to be lowered.

When flown with the national banner of other countries, each flag must be displayed from a separate pole of the same height. Each flag should be the same size. They should be raised and lowered simultaneously. The flag of one nation may not be displayed above that of another nation in time of peace.

The flag should be raised briskly and lowered slowly and ceremoniously.

Ordinarily it should be displayed only between sunrise and sunset, although the Flag Code permits night time display "when a patriotic effect is desired." Similarly, the flag should be displayed only when the weather is fair, except when an all-weather flag is displayed. (By presidential proclamation and law,the flag is displayed continuously at certain honored locations such as the United States Marine Corps Memorial in Arlington and Lexington Green.)

It should be illuminated if displayed at night.

The flag of the United States of America is saluted as it is hoisted and lowered. The salute is held until the flag is unsnapped from the halyard or through the last note of music, whichever is longer.

Displaying the flag indoors

The union is always in the upper left corner. When on display, the flag is accorded the place of honor, always positioned to its own right. Place it to the speaker's right, the audience's left, in a staging area or sanctuary. Other flags should be to the speaker's left.

The flag of the United States of America should be at the center and at the highest point of the group when a number of flags of states, localities, or societies are grouped for display.

When one flag is used with the flag of the United States of America and the staffs are crossed, the flag of the United States is placed on its own right with its staff in front of the other flag. When the flag is displayed against a wall vertically or horizontally, its union (stars) should be at the top, to the flag'sown right, and to the observer's left.

Parading and saluting the flag

When carried in a procession, the flag should be to the right of the marchers.

When other flags are carried, the flag of the United States may be centered in front of the others or carried to their right. When the flag passes in a procession, or when it is hoisted or lowered, all should face the flag and salute.

To salute, all persons come to attention. Those in uniform give the appropriate formal salute.

Members of the Armed Forces and veterans who are present but not in uniform may render the military salute.

Citizens not in uniform salute by placing their right hand over the heart and men with head cover should remove it and hold it to left shoulder, hand over the heart.

Citizens who are not veterans or members of the armed services should not render the military salute.

Citizens of other countries present should stand at attention.

All such conduct toward the flag in a moving column should be rendered at the moment the flag passes.

Pledge of allegiance and national anthem

When reciting the Pledge of Allegiance, all present should stand at attention facing the flag with their right hand over their heart, with the exception of those in uniform who shall salute.
   When the national anthem is played or sung:

1.   Designation: The composition consisting of the words and music known as the Star-Spangled Banner is the national anthem.
2.   ***Conduct During Playing: During a rendition of the national anthem:***
    1.   When the flag is displayed:
        a)   individuals in uniform should give the military salute at the first note of the anthem and maintain that position until the last note;
        b)   members of the Armed Forces and veterans who are present but not in uniform may render the military salute in the manner provided for individuals in uniform; and
        c)   all other persons present should face the flag and stand at attention with their right hand over the heart, and men not in uniform, if applicable, should remove their headdress with their right hand and hold it at the left shoulder, the hand being over the heart; and
    2.   When the flag is not displayed, all present should face toward the music and act in the same manner they would if the flag were displayed.

The flag in mourning

The flag, as draped over President John F. Kennedy's coffin at his state funeral. To place the flag at half-staff (or half-mast, on ships), hoist it to the peak for an instant and lower it to a position half way between the top and bottom of the staff.

The flag is to be raised again to the peak for a moment before it is lowered.

On Memorial Day, the flag is displayed at half-staff until noon and at full staff from noon to sunset.

The flag is to be flown at half-staff in mourning for the death of designated, principal government leaders.

The flag is to be flown at half-staff for thirty days in mourning for the death of the current or former President of the United States.

The U.S. flag is otherwise flown at half-staff (or half-mast, on ships) only when directed by the President of the United States, a state governor (within that state), or the mayor of Washington, *(within the district).*

When used to cover a casket or coffin as a pall, the flag should be placed with the union at the head and over the left shoulder. It should not be lowered into the grave; it is also to be removed before the casket is set for cremation. It is considered a proper sign of courtesy to salute a casket covered with the American flag as the pall (in military and state funerals) at the proper time.

The U.S. flag is to be flown half-staff on Patriot Day (September 11).

Prohibitions

The code prohibits certain uses of the flag; these are enumerated under section eight, and include:

- The flag should never be displayed upside down except as a sign of distress.
- The flag should never touch anything beneath it.
- The flag should never be worn or used as bedding or drapery.
- The flag must always be allowed to fall free and never displayed furled.
- The flag must not be marked with any insignia, letter, word, signature, picture or drawing.
- The flag may not be used for any advertising purposes; no advertising may be attached to a pole flying a flag.

- The image of the flag may not be printed, embroidered or otherwise impressed on anything designed for temporary use and discard. This includes napkins, paper plates and cups, packaging or stamps. (Exception: USA First-Class stamp, 41-cent 2007.)
- No part of the flag should ever be used as a costume or athletic uniform; flag patches are allowed as part of the uniform of a federal, state, civic or patriotic organization. http://en.wikipedia. org/wiki/United_States_Flag_Code

For those of you who dishonor our flag, I say, "shame on you." Recently a veteran returning from a nine-month deployment from Afghanistan received a notice from his landlord in Salem, Virginia asking him to remove a cup full of dirt from his back patio with a small American Flag planted in the dirt. "We need your help to keep our community one of the best in Salem." was what the notice read." Although the Soldier explained that "I like to keep a flag on display in honor of those who have died fighting for our freedom." apparently the landlord felt it was offensive. I do hope this Soldier was able to find another place to live.

XVI

Congress–Pork and Game

O bama is not a leader, but he is very good at one thing. He can convince a fed-up citizenry to be angrier at the other guy than they are at him. Or he can impress the media with the idea that he's outmaneuvering the other guy politically to the degree that they praise him for his shrewdness. It is a game. And when you are as good at the political game as he is, I guess you do not have to be a good leader. The public does not make demands upon you. They are sold on your vision and they demand that Congress support your agenda. In Obama's case, America does not have a clue what Obama's agenda is because he does not express what his agenda is most of the time. We hear him speak about a balanced approach, but to us that would mean a reduced deficit and spending cuts. However, we have learned that Obama does not intend either one. He has no intention of cutting spending and has never proposed a tax increase that makes the smallest dent in the massive deficit. This is why we do not have leadership. If he made an attempt to come up with a Plan, Congress might not like it, but they would feel compelled to support it.

So, since Obama has no leadership, he must play the media for cover. Dictators must maintain absolute power and the media is the only way he has of doing this. He is lousy at his job as President, so he can only maintain his power through the media. He is not respected as an individual leader. The office of the Presidency will always be respected in this Country, but there is a difference between the man and the office. There is a distinction between the two. Just because you sit behind the desk does not give you respect. Just because you were elected to do a job does not give you respect. You must be able to do that job and earn the *respect of the citizenry.*

Now we come to our Congress of the United States; the supposed Leaders of our Country. I am talking about all the pork that our Legislators add to every Bill. When legislators do notice a particular project and have concerns about it, they are often reluctant to object, because they may have legislation or projects of their own that they do not want to put at risk. When are they going to start investigating, or stop adding pork altogether. They hated Bush because he would veto Bills that had pork added to them. That practice needs to go into effect again.

One Congressman recommended requiring that all funding earmarked for individual projects be listed clearly in publicly available reports before the overall funding bill could be voted on by Congress. That would force proponents to justify publicly their provisions for special projects, and would help ensure that fewer wasteful projects will pass. Sunshine is still the best disinfectant for wasteful proposals. I agree.

But every bill ends up quadruple its size because every Congressman wants to add a benefit for his constituent. Congress can reduce pork any time it wants to. I do not recommend reducing it. I recommend eliminating it altogether.

What I do not like is the political aspect of pork. To run for office, a Congressman needs money, and that money usually comes in the form of campaign contributions from these special interest groups. And they are not charities. They expect something back in return, and the way for members of Congress to accomplish that recompense is through pork. Pork has cost the nation 241 billion dollars since 1991, not exactly a meager sum of money in a country whose deficit is currently skyrocketing. The problem is the money is spread out among the tax payers.

Pork and Congress accounts for a great deal of our deficit. In 2006, one bill included $13.5 million for an Irish group that funds the World Toilet Summit, $1 million for water-free urinals, $500,000 for a teapot museum; this all payable by our taxpayers. Alaska takes the cake (or bacon) as the most pork-laden state. Congress has earmarked $325 million, or about $490 per capita, for projects in the sparsely populated state, down from $985 in 2005. Hawaii, at $378 per capita, and the District of Columbia, at $182, are next on the list. "Alaska's drop can be attributed to Sen. Ted Stevens' descent from the throne as Senate Appropriations Committee Chairman," Citizens Against Government Waste said.

Although Republicans agreed to ban earmarking earlier this year, a practice which in many ways has become shorthand for wasteful government spending and shady politics, denied the use of their time-honored negotiating tool, however, legislators are beginning to exploit a loophole in the ban by turning to a far more obscure strategy to seek funding for their constituencies, one that is appropriately being referred to as "phonemarking."

With earmarks, members of Congress tuck pet projects — such as funding for roads or research in their districts — into a piece of legislation in exchange for their vote.

With phonemarking, legislators bypass the open process of adding requests to bills and instead use their clout to call federal agencies directly and request grants for their constituencies. www.kcet.org/shows/.../earmark-ban-makes-congressional-pork-hard-to... Congressmen have learned that pork can also help them and as disgusting as it is, it is not illegal. Some arranged for improvements to areas near property they owned; others sent money to organizations they would later go to work for after leaving office. Congress literally makes its own rules with reference to earmarks.

In my book, Soundoff, I gave my opinion on Congress and how they cannot make a decision without adding a lot of pork or lining their own pockets. We try to change out some of the old ones and add a few new ones and hope they will change, but the old ones just show the new members "how it is done," and more of our money is wasted.

For example, Congress just passed a bill to help the Hurricane Sandy victims in New York and New Jersey. Naturally, the Media did not report anything about the pork that this bill contained, so I will tell you about it here.

"The pork-barrel feast includes more than $8 million to buy cars and equipment for the Homeland Security and Justice Departments. It also included a whopping $150 million for the National Oceanic and Atmospheric Administration to dole out to fisheries in Alaska and $2 million for the Smithsonian Institution to repair museum roofs in DC. Another $13 billion would go to "mitigation" projects to prepare for future storms. Other big-ticket items in the bill include $207 million for the VA Manhattan Medical Center; $41 million to fix up eight military bases along the storm's path, including Guantanamo Bay, Cuba; $4 million for repairs at Kennedy Space Center in Florida; $3.3 million for the Plum Island Animal Disease Center and $1.1 million to repair national cemeteries." Now what does any of this have to do with taking care of the Sandy victims?[62]

None of these things have anything to do with helping Sandy victims, yet they are all part of the Sandy relief package. How is giving $150 million to fisheries in Alaska supposed to help someone in New Jersey or New York who lost his home? How is spending money to fix up Gitmo going to help a business in New York whose building got destroyed by the hurricane? Or spending millions to help repair damages at the space center in Florida going to help a family in New Jersey that lost their home? This is why it takes so long to get anything done in Congress. They have to make all of these deals before they can get anything accomplished. You scratch my back and I will scratch yours next time or on the next bill that comes up. It just goes on and on. It is how it is done in Washington. They never do anything just because it is the right thing to do. They do it to make the deal. If we could only find out the amount of pork that goes on in every bill they pass, at election time we would get rid of every one of them, or would you? Would you just bury your head in the sand like you did on the last election because you do not really care or pay any attention to what is going on in the world; you do not listen to the news, you do not read a book, you just come home tired from your

---

62   http://politicaloutcast.com/2012/12/obamas-sandy-relief-bill-filled-with-pork-barrel-projects/

day at work and either play computer games, answer a few emails, post on Facebook or twitter, get on your cell phone, and then go to bed? That is how it is done in Washington, DC. If the Senator from Alaska will vote for this Bill, we will give him $150 Million for the fisheries in Alaska. Whoever is sponsoring the Smithsonian Bill will get his $2 Million if he votes for this Sandy Bill. And so it goes on until there are enough votes to pass the Sandy Bill.

Does anyone else get upset with our Government and what they do behind your back? We vote them in with a certain amount of trust to do what is right for our country and look at what they do. They do this on every bill that they pass. This is not the only bill they have done this on. They cannot seem to help themselves. They cannot do anything without adding pork to it. They just have to make a deal out of everything. Why? Because that many Senators and Representatives cannot agree on any one thing. The conversation does not begin with where do you stand this Bill, but how much do you need to vote with us on this Bill. Can you possibly imagine how many deals and how much pork is going into raising the taxes on the year end budget? We talk about how much money Obama spends. Well how about how much money Congress spends? We talk about budgets and Obama being the big spender. Look at how much money Congress spends on every Bill they pass just on pork. America cannot afford Congress.[63]

We have elected a Republican Congress that has no gonads. They might as well be Democrats. They cave in on every issue before Congress. They were put in office to do the work of the American people, but so far have done nothing. They took the oath of office saying they would listen to the American people and they would be honest American Citizens. Not one of them has done so. Nearly every one of them has become a Congressman for the purpose of the prestige of the office and having the privilege of a lifetime pension after a six-year term in office. Not one can give an honest vote without adding pork to a bill, or asking for a future favor. That is how it is done. The buck never stops. It is always the art of the deal. It

---

[63] http://politicaloutcast.com/2012/12/obamas-sandy-relief-bill-filled-with-pork-barrel-projects/#ixzz 2FifpYx2l

is the art of the corruption. If America really knew what was going on in Washington, every American would puke. America does not want to know what is going on in Washington. America hides from Washington. America does not listen to the news at night. America does not want to read the Bills or listen to what is going on in the House and the Senate and behind closed doors. They want to be able to Trust the elected legislators. But most do not. They make a great public showing through their lying eyes.

Even when you get an email from a Congressman and they tell you they are fighting for a cause, they want a contribution from you.

What hypocrisy! They are elected to do a job and they are pandering on the internet instead of doing that job.

Congress should keep an eye on Obama and all of his Executive Orders. The Republicans are not saying anything about the Executive Orders.

"If you've enjoyed the fiscal cliff political theater that has consumed Washington over the past few months, you are going to love 2013. Yes, the White House and Congress did finally agree on a deal that prevented about $4 trillion of a scheduled $4.6 trillion tax hike, but there are many fiscal fights still scheduled to occur throughout the New Year.

'First, in about six weeks, the Treasury Department will reach its legal borrowing limit. At that point, Treasury Secretary Tim Geithner will not be allowed to finance government spending by issuing new debt and will have to pick and choose which of the Federal Government's many spending obligations it will and will not pay. Contrary to what some on the left believe, the 14th Amendment of the U.S. Constitution does not authorize Geithner to ignore the debt limit. What it does do is obligate him to make sure the Federal government pays off its lenders first. And since the Federal government is constantly taking in more money in taxes than it owes in debt service, there is zero danger the U.S. will default on its debt. But everyone else who gets payments from the Federal government will be in danger of not getting paid. Since the Federal Government plays such a large role in economic affairs this will create chaos in the U.S. economy until the issue is resolved.

'Then, after the debt limit is settled, Congress and the White House will have to decide how to resolve the scheduled $1.2 trillion in scheduled spending sequester cuts that were passed into law the last time the debt limit was raised and were delayed for two months as part of last night's fiscal cliff deal. Failing to resolve those scheduled spending cuts would again force the Obama administration to stop making payments to many Americans expecting that income.

'Then, after the debt limit and sequester is settled, Congress and the White House will have to pass legislation authorizing government funding for the next year. The Democratically controlled Senate has not passed a budget since ObamaCare became law and as a result the Federal government has been operating on a series of continuing resolutions ever since. The last one, passed in September 2012, expires March 27th. If no agreement is made on Federal spending before that date, the Federal government will be forced to shut down.

'How each of these next fiscal crisis moments is resolved will go a long way in determining who got the better bargain in the fiscal cliff deal. If Obama is again able to raise taxes in any of the next three fiscal events, then this fiscal cliff deal looks great for the White House. They will have secured a $600 billion down payment on actually paying for the Obama welfare state and can slowly build to the $1.6 trillion he initially asked for.

'But if Republicans hold firm, and do not agree to any new tax hikes, then this deal looks like a disaster for the White House. They will have blown a once in a generation opportunity to raise taxes by trillions of dollars on the American people and will be forced to pare back Obama's previous historic spending gains.

'How anything else gets done in this bitter environment (on guns, immigration, climate change, etc.) is hard to see."[64]

We have refused to honor God, and in so doing, we open the doors to hatred and violence. When a tragedy occurs, Congress seeks to pass more restrictive laws that contribute to erode away our personal and private liberties. We do not need more restrictive laws. No amount of gun laws can stop someone that spends months planning

---

[64] http://washingtonexaminer.com/morning-examiner-the-obama-new-normal/ article/2517347?custom_click=rss#.UOyZQcVXnUI

a massacre. "Experts have told us that society is sick. Their panaceas have treated human frailty with infusions of low-income housing, welfare payments, integrated education, and psychological conditioning. But we are learning that this is not the total answer. The world does need changing, society needs changing, the nation needs changing, but we never will change it until we ourselves are changed. And we never will change until we look into the mirror of our own soul and face with candor what we are inside. Then freely acknowledge that there is a defect in human nature, a built-in waywardness that comes from man's natural rebellion against God. I am not preaching now, just trying to give you an understanding of what makes you tick. But I also expect to show you that, in the end, you can find your answers only in a personal relationship with God." (Billy Graham)

It is only the Democratic Congressmen that are worried about whether they will get re-elected that you can count on when it comes to voting against Dianne Feinstein's bill for very strict gun control. Those are the ones that Harry Reid will not be able to convince to come to his side.

Now you have Congress fighting over whether or not to allow us to keep our guns. Of special interest, a state senator, R. C. Soles (D-NC), a long time anti-gun advocate shot one of two intruders at his home. The injuries were not life threatening and Soles was not arrested, but I find it interesting that a man that has made a career of being against gun ownership for the general public did not hesitate to defend himself with his own gun when he believed he was in immediate danger and he was the victim. Can we take a poll of all of the Congressmen in Washington to see how many of them own guns? How many of them do as I say, not as I do? Do they think their lives are more valuable than your life or mine?

I make no secret about my feelings that most Congressmen are corrupt morons. There are 535 Congressmen and you would think some of them could get it right for this Country. The only time they start to act is when it is time to run for office again. From the time they are elected until it is re-election time, the public hears nothing from them unless they want to toot their horn to get a vote.

Our Social Security was established in 1935 and Congress has had 74 years to build it into a major fund for the senior citizens, but instead they have used it as an incoming tax payable to the United States government for their spending purposes. They have literally stolen the retirement funds of the elderly American people from right under our noses and they continue to do so. You put Bernie Madoff in jail for doing the very thing that you have done and you should get the very same sentence that he received. Worse yet, you continue to spend the future retirement funds of The People to keep the present retirees afloat and at some point those will run out.

Yet you just keep spending and spending, not worrying about where the money is coming from.

$1 trillion is confiscated each year and transferred to "the poor" and they only want more. When are you going to reform that policy. There needs to be welfare reform. You need to get rid of the Obama-phones. You need to get rid of the EBT cards. You need to reform the Unemployment system. The poor is not so poor anymore. They are better off being dependent on the government than getting a job.

Medicare and Medicaid were established in 1965. You have had 44 years to get it right and they are broke. You are not paying attention and someone is not doing their job. There needs to be reform in these departments.

Fannie Mae and Freddie Mac are both broke. All of the years of trying to get it right just have not worked either.

The Department of Energy needs to be shut down. It was created in 1977 and the only thing it has done is create laws to shut down businesses. It has 16,000 employees with a budget of $24 billion a year and we import more oil than ever before. All they have done is shut down coal mines.

You have failed in every "government service" you have rammed down our throats while overspending our tax dollars. You even wanted Americans to believe you could be trusted with government-run health care system where "you have to vote on it" to know what is in it. And it was not good enough for Congress. They have their own health care package.

XVII

Impeachment

On January 15, 2013, Articles of Impeachment were filed against Barack Hussein Obama by Alexander Emric Jones. "The time has now come for a bill of impeachment to be introduced and debated in Congress. Obama's crimes are public, and the debate in the House will serve as a court in which to display the tyrannical activities of President Obama and his cohorts. As in the case of Richard Nixon, the exposure of Obama's crimes may cause him to resign in disgrace. If he does not step down, the full House will then vote to begin the impeachment trial in the US Senate. The time has now come to make your decision – to *stand up to evil or get on your knees as a willing slave." Congressman Steve Stockman has pledged to stand behind*

Citizen Jones and said in his statement that "The President's actions are an existential threat to this nation." "The right of the people to keep and bear arms is what has kept this nation free and secure for over 200 years. The very purpose of the Second Amendment is to stop the government from disallowing people the means to defend themselves against tyranny. Any proposal to abuse executive power and infringe upon gun rights must be repelled with the stiffest legislative force possible. I will seek to thwart this action by any means necessary, including but not limited to eliminating funding for implementation, defunding the White House, and even filing articles of impeachment."

He has aided America's enemies, violating his oath, by sending funds to insurgents in Syria who are being commanded by Al-Qaeda terrorists.

He has violated federal law by overseeing a cover-up surrounding Operation Fast and Furious, the transfer of guns to Mexican drug cartels direct from the federal government.

He has lied to the American people by overseeing a cover-up of the Benghazi attack which directly led to the deaths of four American citizens. The cover-up has been called "Obama's Watergate," yet four months after the incident, no one in the administration has been held accountable.

He has brazenly undermined the power of Congress by insisting his authority came from the United Nations Security Council prior to the attack on Libya and that Congressional approval was not necessary. "I don't even have to get to the Constitutional question," said Obama. This is an act that "constitutes an impeachable high crime and misdemeanor under article II, section 4 of the Constitution," according to Congressman Walter Jones.

He has ignored Congressional rejection of the cybersecurity bill and instead indicated he will pursue an unconstitutional executive order.

He has signed into law the National Defense Authorization Act which includes provisions that permit the abduction and military detention without trial of U.S. citizens, violating Habeas Corpus. Despite Obama claiming he would not use the provisions to incarcerate U.S. citizens, it was his administration that specifically demanded these powers be included in the final NDAA bill.

He has enacted universal health care mandates that force Americans to buy health insurance, a clear violation of the Constitution in exceeding congressional power to regulate interstate commerce. Obama has also handed out preferential waivers to corporations friendly to his administration.

He has declared war on America's coal industry by promising to bankrupt any company that attempts to build a new coal plant while using unconstitutional EPA regulations to strangle competition, ensuring Americans see their energy costs rise year after year.

He has violated the Constitution's Takings and Due Process Clauses when he bullied the secured creditors of automaker Chrysler into accepting 30 cents on the dollar while politically connected labor unions and preferential others received better deals.

He has violated Article II of the Constitution by using signing statements as part of his executive usurpation of power.[65]

Florida Republican Congressman Trey Radel is also suggesting Obama should be impeached. In a statement, Radel said "It is one of those times in our history, we are at this breaking point," Radel added, going on to explain, "We have completely lost our checks and balances in this country, the Congress needs to hold the president accountable for the decisions that he's making right now, and that why again, I would say that all options should be on the table."

In 2011, Bruce Fein, a prominent libertarian constitutional lawyer and civil libertarian drafted an article of impeachment against President Obama over his attack on Libya. "He's been more bold than any other president," said Fein, who said Obama has failed to secure congressional approval for his military action in a much more brazen way than previous administrations. "If he can wipe out the war powers authorization, why can't he wipe out Congress's authority to spend?" asked Fein. "If we're going to be a government of laws, and not descend into empire, this is Caesar crossing the Rubicon."

In March of 2012, An American military attack on Syria could effectively lead to the impeachment of President Barack Obama. Congressmen say that any war without congressional authorization would be "unconstitutional". Republican Representative Walter B. Jones Jr. has come up with the resolution demanding Obama's impeachment in case his administration starts another military action without the approval of Congress. This came as a reaction to the American Defense Secretary Leon Panetta announcing that in order to carry out the offensive, the US military needs permission

---

[65]   http://www.teaparty.org/congressman-warns-obama-impeach-you-18676/

from the UN and NATO alone. Jones's resolution states that the prime authority to rule on the attack is the US Congress, but not international bodies be it NATO or UN.

Although Petitions are filed, why do we not hear anything further about them? What happens to them? Does Congress just not act on them?

Some of those who have broached the subject include Reps. Trent Franks, R-Ariz.; Walter Jones, R-N.C.; former Rep. Ron Paul, R-Texas; former Rep. Dennis Kucinich, D-Ohio; Fox News' Mike Huckabee; former assistant U.S. attorney Andrew McCarthy; left-leaning investigative reporter Dave Lindorff; talk-radio host Mark Levin; former House Speaker and presidential candidate Newt Gingrich; author and columnist Pat Buchanan and others.

Only two United States presidents have ever been impeached by the House of Representatives: Andrew Johnson and Bill Clinton. Both presidents were acquitted in the Senate. President Richard Nixon resigned before the full House had voted on his impeachment.

If you want to sign Articles of Impeachment, you may go to the following site[66] and then after you have read the Articles, if you wish to sign them, click on "Sign the Petition" and it will take you to another window. Or, if you do not have a computer, this is what the Articles of Impeachment say:

Article Of Impeachment Of President Barack Hussein Obama

RESOLVED, That Barack Hussein Obama, President of the United States, is impeached for high crimes and misdemeanors, and that the following article of impeachment to be exhibited to the Senate:

ARTICLE OF IMPEACHMENT EXHIBITED BY THE HOUSE OF REPRESENTATIVES OF THE UNITED STATES OF AMERICA IN THE NAME OF ITSELF AND OF ALL OF THE PEOPLE OF THE UNITED STATES OF AMERICA, AGAINST BARACK HUSSEIN OBAMA, PRESIDENT

---

[66]   http://www.impeachobamacampaign.com/ articlesofimpeachment/

OF THE UNITED STATES OF AMERICA, IN MAINTENANCE AND SUPPORT OF ITS IMPEACHMENT AGAINST HIM FOR HIGH CRIMES AND MISDEMEANORS IN USURPING THE EXCLUSIVE PREROGATIVE OF CONGRESS TO COMENCE WAR UNDER ARTICLE 1, SECTION 8,CLAUSE 11 OF THE CONSTITUTION.

Article I

In his conduct of the office of President of the United States, Barack Hussein Obama, in violation of his constitutional oath faithfully to execute the office of President of the United States and, to the best of his ability, preserve, protect, and defend the Constitution of the United States, and in violation of his constitutional duty to take care that the laws be faithfully executed, has usurped the exclusive power of Congress to initiate war under Article I, section 8, clause 11 of the United States Constitution by unilaterally commencing war against the Republic of Libya on March 19, 2011, declaring that Congress is powerless to constrain his conduct of the war, and claiming authority in the future to commence war unilaterally to advance whatever he ordains is in the national interest. By so doing and declaring, Barack Hussein Obama has mocked the rule of law, endangered the very existence of the Republic and the liberties of the people, and perpetrated an impeachable high crime and misdemeanor as hereinafter elaborated.

I.   The Impeachment Power

    1.   Article II, Section IV of the United States Constitution provides: "The President, Vice President and all civil Officers of the United States, shall be removed from Office on Impeachment for, and Conviction of, Treason, Bribery, or other high Crimes and Misdemeanors." According to James Madison's Records of the Convention,

2. 2:550; Madison, 8 Sept., Mr. George Mason objected to an initial proposal to confine impeachable offenses to treason or bribery: Why is the provision restrained to Treason & bribery only? Treason as defined in the Constitution will not reach many great and dangerous offences. Hastings is not guilty of Treason. Attempts to subvert the Constitution may not be Treason as above defined–As bills of attainder which have saved the British Constitution are forbidden, it is the more necessary to extend: the power of impeachments.

3. Delegates to the Federal Convention voted overwhelmingly to include "high crimes and misdemeanors" in Article II, Section IV of the United States Constitution specifically to ensure that "attempts to subvert the Constitution" would fall within the universe of impeachable offences. Id.

4. Alexander Hamilton, a delegate to the Federal Convention, characterized impeachable offenses in Federalist 65 as, "offenses which proceed from the misconduct of public men, or in other words, from the violation or abuse of some public trust. They are of a nature which with peculiar propriety may be denominated political, as they relate chiefly to injuries done to society itself."

5. In 1974, the House Judiciary Committee voted three articles of impeachment against then President Richard M. Nixon for actions "subversive of constitutional government."

6. Father of the Constitution, James Madison, observed that, "Of all the enemies of public liberty, war is, perhaps, the most to be dreaded, because it comprises and develops the germ of every other.... War is the true nurse of executive aggrandizement."

7. James Madison also instructed that "no nation could preserve its freedom in the midst of continual warfare."

8. The exclusive congressional power to commence war under Article I, section VIII, clause XI of the Constitution is the pillar of the Republic and the greatest constitutional

guarantor of individual liberty, transparency, and government frugality.

II.   The "Declare War" Clause

9. Article I, Section VIII, Clause XI of the United States Constitution provides: "The Congress shall have the power ... To declare War, grant Letters of Marque and Reprisal, and make Rules concerning Captures on Land and Water;"

10. Article II, Section II, Clause I of the United States Constitution provides:"The President shall be Commander in Chief of the Army and Navy of the United States, and of the Militia of the several States, when called into the actual Service of the United States."

11. The authors of the United States Constitution manifestly intended Article I, Section VIII, Clause XI to fasten exclusive responsibility and authority on the Congress to decide whether to undertake offensive military action.

12. The authors of the United States Constitution believed that individual liberty and the Republic would be endangered by fighting too many wars, not too few.

13. The authors of the United States Constitution understood that to aggrandize power and to leave a historical legacy, the executive in all countries chronically inflates danger manifold to justify warfare.

14. John Jay, the first Chief Justice of the United States, in Federalist 4 noted:

    [A]bsolute monarchs will often make war when their nations are to get nothing by it, but for the purposes and objects merely personal, such as thirst for military glory, revenge for personal affronts, ambition, or private compacts to aggrandize or support their particular families or partisans. These and a variety of other motives, which affect only the mind of the sovereign, often lead him to engage in wars not sanctified by justice or the voice and interests of his people.

15. Alexander Hamilton explained in Federalist 69 that the president's Commander-in-Chief authority

...would be nominally the same with that of the King of Great Britain, but in substance much inferior to it. It would amount to nothing more than the supreme command and direction of the military and naval forces, as first general and admiral of the confederacy; while that of the British king extends to the declaring of war, and to the raising and regulating of fleets and armies; all which by the constitution under consideration would appertain to the Legislature.

16. In a written exchange with Alexander Hamilton under the pseudonym Helvidius, James Madison wrote:

In no part of the constitution is more wisdom to be found, than in the clause which confides the question of war or peace to the legislature, and not to the executive department. Beside the objection to such a mixture to heterogeneous powers, the trust and the temptation would be too great for any one man; not such as nature may offer as the prodigy of many centuries, but such as may be expected in the ordinary successions of magistracy. War is in fact the true nurse of executive aggrandizement. In war, a physical force is to be created; and it is the executive will, which is to direct it. In war, the public treasures are to be unlocked; and it is the executive hand which is to dispense them. In war, the honours and emoluments of office are to be multiplied; and it is the executive patronage under which they are to be enjoyed. It is in war, finally, that laurels are to be gathered, and it is the executive brow they are to encircle. The strongest passions and most dangerous weaknesses of the human breast; ambition, avarice, vanity, the honourable or venial love of fame, are all in conspiracy against the desire and duty of peace.

17. James Madison also wrote as Helvidius to Alexander Hamilton:

    Those who are to conduct a war cannot in the nature of things, be proper or safe judges, whether a war ought to be commenced, continued, or concluded. They are barred from the latter functions by a great principle in free government, analogous to that which separates the sword from the purse, or the power of executing from the power of enacting laws.

18. On June 29, 1787, at the Federal Convention, James Madison explained that an executive crowned with war powers invites tyranny and the reduction of citizens to vassalage:

    In time of actual war, great discretionary powers are constantly given to the Executive Magistrate. Constant apprehension of War, has the same tendency to render the head too large for the body. A standing military force, with an overgrown Executive will not long be safe companions to liberty. The means of defence agst. foreign danger, have been always the instruments of tyranny at home. Among the Romans it was a standing maxim to excite a war, whenever a revolt was apprehended. Throughout all Europe, the armies kept up under the pretext of defending, have enslaved the people.

19. In a letter dated April 4, 1798, James Madison wrote to Thomas Jefferson:

    The constitution supposes, what the History of all Governments demonstrates, that the Executive is the branch of power most interested in war, & most prone to it. It has accordingly with studied care, vested the question of war in the Legislature. But the Doctrines lately advanced strike at the root of all these provisions, and will deposit the peace of the Country in that Department which the Constitution distrusts as most ready without cause to renounce it. For if the opinion of the President not the facts & proofs themselves are to sway the judgment of Congress, in declaring war, and if the President in the recess of Congress create a foreign mission, appoint the minister, & negociate a War Treaty, without the possibility of a check even from the Senate, until the measures present alternatives overruling the freedom of its judgment; if again a Treaty when made obliges the Legislature to declare war contrary to its judgment, and in pursuance of the same doctrine, a law declaring war, imposes a like moral obligation, to grant the requisite supplies until it be formally repealed with the consent of the President & Senate, it is evident that the people are cheated out of the best ingredients in their Government, the safeguards of peace which is the greatest of their blessings.

20. During the Pennsylvania Convention to ratify the Constitution, James Wilson, a future Justice of the United States Supreme Court, observed:
This system will not hurry us into war; it is calculated to guard against it. It will not be in the power of a single man, or a single body of men, to involve us in such distress; for the important power of declaring war is vested in the legislature at large: this declaration must he made with the concurrence of the House of Representatives: from this circumstance we may draw a certain conclusion that nothing but our national interest can draw us into a war.

21. In 1793, President George Washington, who presided over the Federal Convention, wrote to South Carolina Governor William Moultrie in regards to a prospective counter-offensive against the American Indian Creek Nation: "The Constitution vests the power of declaring war with Congress, therefore no offensive expedition of importance can be undertaken until after they have deliberated upon the subject, and authorized such a measure."

22. President Thomas Jefferson, who served as Secretary of State under President Washington, in a statement before Congress regarding Tripoli and the Barbary Pirates, deemed himself "unauthorized by the Constitution, without the sanction of Congress, to go beyond the line of defense."

He amplified: "I communicate [to the Congress] all material information on this subject, that in the exercise of this important function confided by the Constitution to the Legislature exclusively their judgment may form itself on a knowledge and consideration of every circumstance of weight."

23. In a message to Congress in December, 1805 regarding potential military action to resolve a border dispute with Spain, President Thomas Jefferson acknowledged that "Congress alone is constitutionally invested with the power of changing our condition from peace to war, I have thought it my duty to await their authority for using force." He requested Congressional authorization for offensive military action, even short of war, elaborating:
Formal war is not necessary—it is not probable it will follow; but the protection of our citizens, the spirit and honor of our country, require that force should be interposed to a certain degree. It will probably contribute to advance the object of peace.

But the course to be pursued will require the command of means which it belongs to Congress exclusively to yield or deny. To them I communicate every fact material for their information, and the documents necessary to enable them to judge for themselves. To their wisdom, then, I look for the course I am to pursue; and will pursue, with sincere zeal, that which they shall approve.

24. In his War Message to Congress on June 1, 1812, President James Madison reaffirmed that the shift in language from make to declare in Article I, Section VIII, Clause XI of the United States Constitution authorized at the Constitutional convention did not empower the Executive to involve the United States military in any action aside from defense against an overt attack. Although President Madison was convinced that Great Britain had undertaken acts of war against the United States, he nevertheless

maintained that he could not respond with military force without congressional authorization. He proclaimed:

We behold, in fine, on the side of Great Britain, a state of war against the United States, and on the side of the United States a state of peace toward Great Britain.

Whether the United States shall continue passive under these progressive usurpations and these accumulating wrongs, or, opposing force to force in defense of their national rights, shall commit a just cause into the hands of the Almighty Disposer of Events, avoiding all connections which might entangle it in the contest or views of other powers, and preserving a constant readiness to concur in an honorable re-establishment of peace and friendship, is a solemn question which the Constitution wisely confides to the legislative department of the Government. In recommending it to their early deliberations I am happy in the assurance that the decision will be worthy the enlightened and patriotic councils of a virtuous, a free, and a powerful nation.

25. In his Records of the Convention, 2:318; Madison, 17 Aug., James Madison wrote that the power "To declare war" had been vested in the Congress in lieu of the power "To make war" to leave to the Executive "the power to repel sudden attacks."

26. Mr. Elbridge Gerry "never expected to hear in a republic a motion to empower the Executive alone to declare war," but still moved with Mr. Madison "to insert declare—in place of make" in Article I, Section VIII, Clause XI. Id.

27. Mr. George Mason was against "giving the power of war to the Executive, because not safely to be trusted with it; or to the Senate, because not so constructed as to be entitled to it. He was for clogging rather than facilitating war; but for facilitating peace." Yet Mr. Mason "preferred declare to make." Id.

28. Mr. Roger Sherman "thought [the proposal] stood very well. The Executive shd. be able to repel and not to commence war." Id.

29. Delegates to the Federal Convention overwhelmingly approved the motion to insert "declare—in place of make," to deny the Executive power to initiate military action, but to permit the Executive to repel sudden attacks unilaterally. Id.

30. Then Congressman Abraham Lincoln sermonized:
Allow the President to invade a neighboring nation, whenever he shall deem it necessary to repel an invasion, and you allow him to do so, whenever he may choose to say he deems it necessary for such purpose — and you allow him to make war at pleasure.... Study to see if you can fix any limit to his power in this respect, after you have given him so much as you propose. If, to-day, he should choose to say he thinks it necessary to invade Canada, to prevent the British from invading us, how could you stop him? You may say to him, "I see no probability of the British invading us" but he will say to you "be silent; I see it, if you don't."

The provision of the Constitution giving the war-making power to Congress, was dictated, as I understand it, by the following reasons. Kings had always been involving and impoverishing their people in wars, pretending generally, if not always, that the good of the people was the object. This, our Convention understood to be the most oppressive of all Kingly oppressions; and they resolved to so frame the Constitution that no one man should hold the power of bringing this oppression upon us. But your view destroys the whole matter, and places our President where kings have always stood.

31. Crowning the President with unilateral authority to commence war under the banner of anticipatory self-defense, prevention of civilian slaughters, gender discrimination, subjugation of ethnic or religious minorities, or other-

wise would empower the President to initiate war without limit, threatening the very existence of the Republic. Although a benevolent Chief Executive might resist abuse of an unlimited war power, the principle, if ever accepted by Congress, would lie around like a loaded weapon ready for use by any successor craving absolute power.

32. Thomas Paine justly and rightly declared in Common Sense that "in America, the law is king. For as in absolute governments the King is law, so in free countries the law ought to be king; and there ought to be no other."

33. Article 43 Paragraph 3 of the Charter of the United Nations provides that all resolutions or agreements of the United Nations Security Counsel "shall be subject to ratification by the signatory states in accordance with their respective constitutional processes."

34. Article 43 Paragraph 3 of Charter of the United Nations was included specifically to allay concerns that prevented the United States of America from ratifying the League of Nations Treaty in 1919.

35. That treaty risked crowning the President with the counter-constitutional authority to initiate warfare. On November 19, 1919, in Section II of his Reservations with Regard to Ratification of the Versailles Treaty, to preserve the balance of power established by the United States Constitution from executive usurpation, Senator Henry Cabot Lodge resolved as follows:
The United States assumes no obligation to preserve the territorial integrity or political independence of any other country or to interfere in controversies between nations — whether members of the League or not — under the provisions of Article 10, or to employ the military or naval forces of the United States under any article of the treaty for any purpose, unless in any particular case the Congress, which, under the Constitution, has the sole power to declare war or authorize the employment of the

military or naval forces of the United States, shall by act or joint resolution so provide.

The rejection of Lodge's reservations by President Woodrow Wilson and his Senate allies insured defeat of the treaty.

36. Section 2(c) of the War Powers Resolution of 1973 clarifies Presidential authority to undertake military action as follows:

The constitutional powers of the President as Commander-in-Chief to introduce United States Armed Forces into hostilities, or into situations where imminent involvement in hostilities is clearly indicated by the circumstances, are exercised only pursuant to (1) a declaration of war, (2) specific statutory authorization, or (3) a national emergency created by attack upon the United States, its territories or possessions, or its armed forces.

37. In United States v. Smith, 27 F. Cas. 1192 (1806), Supreme Court Justice William Paterson, a delegate to the Federal Convention from New Jersey, wrote on behalf of a federal circuit court:

There is a manifest distinction between our going to war with a nation at peace, and a war being made against us by an actual invasion, or a formal declaration. In the former case it is the exclusive province of Congress to change a state of peace into a state of war.

38. In Geofroy v. Riggs, 133 U.S. 258, 267 (1890), the Supreme Court of the United States held:

The treaty power, as expressed in the Constitution, is in terms unlimited except by those restraints which are found in that instrument against the action of the government or of its departments, and those arising from the nature of the government itself and of that of the States. It would not be contended that it extends so far as to authorize what the Constitution forbids, or a change in the character of the government, or in that of one of the States, or a cession of any portion of the territory of the latter, without its consent.

39. In his concurrence in Youngstown Sheet & Tube Co. v. Sawyer, 343 U.S. 579, 642-643 (1952), which rebuked President Harry Truman's claim of unilateral war powers in the Korean War, Justice Robert Jackson elaborated:
Nothing in our Constitution is plainer than that declaration of a war is entrusted only to Congress. Of course, a state of war may in fact exist without a formal declaration. But no doctrine that the Court could promulgate would seem to me more sinister and alarming than that a President whose conduct of foreign affairs is so largely uncontrolled, and often even is unknown, can vastly enlarge his mastery over the internal affairs of the country by his own commitment of the Nation's armed forces to some foreign venture.

40. All treaties are subservient to the exclusive congressional power to commence war. In Reid v. Covert, 354 U.S. 1, 18 (1957), the United States Supreme Court held:
There is nothing in [the Constitution's text] which intimates that treaties and laws enacted pursuant to them do not have to comply with the provisions of the Constitution. Nor is there anything in the debates which accompanied the drafting and ratification of the Constitution which even suggests such a result.

41. Unconstitutional usurpations by one branch of government of powers entrusted to a coequal branch are not rendered constitutional by repetition. The United States Supreme Court held unconstitutional hundreds of laws enacted by Congress over the course of five decades that included a legislative veto of executive actions in INS v. Chada, 462 U.S. 919 (1982).

42. In their dissent in Hamdi v. Rumsfeld, 542 U.S. 507 (2004), Justices John Paul Stevens and Antonin Scalia recognized the "Founders' general distrust of military power

lodged with the President, including the authority to commence war:

No fewer than 10 issues of the Federalist were devoted in whole or part to allaying fears of oppression from the proposed Constitution's authorization of standing armies in peacetime. Many safeguards in the Constitution reflect these concerns. Congress's authority "[t]o raise and support Armies"was hedged with the proviso that "no Appropriation of Money to that Use shall be for a longer Term than two Years." U.S. Const., Art. 1, §8, cl. 12. Except for the actual command of military forces, all authorization for their maintenance and all explicit authorization for their use is placed in the control of Congress under Article I, rather than the President under Article II. As Hamilton explained, the President's military authority would be "much inferior" to that of the British King… (Citing Federalist 69, Supra.)

43. On December 20, 2007, then Senator Hillary Clinton proclaimed: "The President has the solemn duty to defend our Nation. If the country is under truly imminent threat of attack, of course the President must take appropriate action to defend us. At the same time, the Constitution requires Congress to authorize war. I do not believe that the President can take military action — including any kind of strategic bombing — against Iran without congressional authorization."

44. Then Senator Joseph Biden stated in a speech at the Iowa City Public Library in 2007 regarding potential military action in Iran that unilateral action by the President would be an impeachable offense under the Constitution:

It is precisely because the consequences of war – intended or otherwise – can be so profound and complicated that our Founding Fathers vested in Congress, not the President, the power to initiate war, except to repel an imminent attack on the United States or its citizens.

They reasoned that requiring the President to come to Congress first would slow things down… allow for more careful decision making before sending Americans to fight and die… and ensure broader public support.

The Founding Fathers were, as in most things, profoundly right.

That's why I want to be very clear: if the President takes us to war with Iran without Congressional approval, I will call for his impeachment.

I do not say this lightly or to be provocative. I am dead serious. I have chaired the Senate Judiciary Committee. I still teach constitutional law. I've consulted with some of our leading constitutional scholars. The Constitution is clear. And so am I.

I'm saying this now to put the administration on notice and hopefully to deter the President from taking unilateral action in the last year of his administration.

If war is warranted with a nation of 70 million people, it warrants coming to Congress and the American people first.

45. In a speech on the Senate Floor in 1998, then Senator Joseph Biden maintained: "…the only logical conclusion is that the framers [of the United States Constitution] intended to grant to Congress the power to initiate all hostilities, even limited wars."

46. On December 20, 2007, then Senator Barack Obama informed the Boston Globe, based upon his extensive knowledge of the United States Constitution: "The President does not have power under the Constitution to unilaterally authorize a military attack in a situation that does not involve stopping an actual or imminent threat to the nation."

III.   Usurpation Of The War Power Over Libya

47. President Barack Obama's military attacks against Libya constitute acts of war.

48. Congressman J. Randy Forbes (VA-4) had the following exchange with Secretary of Defense Robert Gates during a March 31, 2011 House Armed Services Committee Hearing on the legality of the present military operation in Libya:

Congressman Forbes: Mr. Secretary, if tomorrow a foreign nation intentionally, for whatever reason, launched a Tomahawk missile into New York City, would that be considered an act of war against the United States?

Secretary Gates: Probably so.

Congressman Forbes: Then I would assume the same laws would apply if we launched a Tomahawk missile at another nation—is that also true?

Secretary Gates: You're getting into constitutional law here and I am no expert on it.

Congressman Forbes: Mr. Secretary, you're the Secretary of Defense. You ought to be an expert on what's an act of war or not. If it's an act of war to launch a Tomahawk missile on New York City would it not also be an act of war to launch a Tomahawk missile by us at another nation?

Secretary Gates: Presumably.

49. Since the passage of United Nations Security Council resolution 1973 on March 19, 2011, the United States has detonated over 200 tomahawk land attack cruise missiles and 455 precision-guided bombs on Libyan soil.

50. Libya posed no actual or imminent threat to the United States when President Obama unleashed Operation Odyssey Dawn.

51. On March 27, 2011, Secretary of Defense Robert Gates stated that Libya never posed an "actual or imminent threat to the United States." He further stated that Libya has never constituted a "vital interest" to the United States.

52. United Nations Security Council resolution 1973 directs an indefinite United States military quagmire in Libya, authorizing "all necessary measures" to protect Libyan civilians, which clearly contemplates removal by force of the murderous regime of Col. Muammar Qadhafi.

53. In a Letter From the President to the Speaker of the House of Representatives and the President Pro Tempore of the Senate sent March 21, 2011, President Barack Obama informed Members of Congress that "U.S. forces have targeted the Qadhafi regime's air defense systems, command and control structures, and other capabilities of Qadhafi's armed forces used to attack civilians and civilian populated areas. We will seek a rapid, but responsible, transition of operations to coalition, regional, or international organizations that are postured to continue activities as may be necessary to realize the objectives of *U.N. Security Council Resolutions 1970 and 1973.*"

54. In his March 21, 2011 letter, President Barack Obama further informed Members of Congress that he opted to take unilateral military action "…in support of international efforts to protect civilians and prevent a humanitarian disaster."

55. President Barack Obama has usurped congressional authority to decide on war or peace with Libya, and has declared he will persist in additional usurpations of the congressional power to commence war whenever he decrees it would advance his idea of the national interest. On March 28, 2011, he declared to Congress and the American people: "I have made it clear that I will never hesitate to use our military swiftly, decisively, and unilaterally when necessary to defend our people, our homeland, our allies, and our core interests" (emphasis added).

56. President Obama's humanitarian justification for war in Libya establishes a threshold that would justify his initiation of warfare in scores of nations around the globe,

including Iran, North Korea, Syria, Sudan, Myanmar, China, Belarus, Zimbabwe, Cuba, and Russia.

57. In Olmstead v. United States, 277 U.S. 438 (1928), Justice Louis D. Brandeis wrote on behalf of a majority of the United States Supreme Court:

Experience should teach us to be most on our guard to protect liberty when the Government's purposes are beneficent. Men born to freedom are naturally alert to repel invasion of their liberty by evil-minded rulers. The greatest dangers to liberty lurk in insidious encroachment by men of zeal, well meaning but without understanding.

58. *President Barack Obama has signed an order, euphemistically named a "Presidential Finding," authorizing covert U.S.* government support for rebel forces seeking to oust Libyan leader Muammar Gaddafi, further entangling the United States in the Libyan conflict, despite earlier promises of restraint. Truth is invariably the first casualty of war.

59. In response to questions by Members of Congress during a classified briefing on March 30, 2011, Secretary of State Hillary Clinton indicated that the President needs no Congressional authorization for his attack on the Libyan nation, and will ignore any Congressional attempt by resolution or otherwise to constrain or halt United States participation in the Libyan war.

60. On March 30, 2011, by persistent silence or otherwise, Secretary Clinton rebuffed congressional inquiries into President Obama's view of the constitutionality of the War Powers Resolution of 1973. She failed to cite a single judicial decision in support of President Obama's recent actions, relying instead on the undisclosed legal opinions of White House attorneys.

61. President Barack Obama, in flagrant violation of his constitutional oath to execute his office as President of the United States and preserve and protect the United States Constitution, has usurped the exclusive authority of Congress to authorize the initiation of war, in that on

March 19, 2011 President Obama initiated an offensive military attack against the Republic of Libya without congressional authorization. In so doing, President Obama has arrested the rule of law, and saluted a vandalizing of the Constitution that will occasion ruination of the Republic, the crippling of individual liberty, and a Leviathan government unless the President is impeached by the House of Representatives and removed from office by the Senate.

In all of this, President Barack Obama has acted in a manner contrary to his trust as President and subversive of constitutional government, to the great prejudice of the cause of law and justice and to the manifest injury of the people of the United States. http://www.impeachobamacampaign.com/articlesofimpeachment/

It really does not matter how many grounds you have for impeachment if you do not have a Congress that will stand up and do their duty. This Congress is afraid of Obama and his henchmen and will do nothing.

XVIII

Constitution

I t grieves me that there are so many that are willing to throw away our Constitution and our Declaration of Independence that our forefathers so craftily created to protect us from such *conditions as those that face us today.*

It grieves me that you do not understand that you are about to thrust away your freedoms that have been enjoyed by Americans for these 200 plus years and you are so totally ignorant of the consequences. If you would only pick up a history book and see what conditions you will be living under if you do not wake up.

It grieves me that so many of you have never read a book, let alone our Constitution, or our Declaration of Independence, or have any idea what they contain.

It grieves me that if they were ripped up today that you think life for you would go on tomorrow as it goes on today and yesterday.

It grieves me that some of you do not even know who the president is, let alone what he is doing to this country.

The Declaration of Independence is a document that sets out all of the reasons why the early settlers came to this country and fought to get away from despotism, and the King of England, and socialism. My book Soundoff contained a copy of the Declaration of Independence and a copy of the Constitution. If I write another book, it will also contain a copy of those important documents and just maybe you will read them. Your future is at stake here.

I ask you to read the Declaration of Independence because it shows you not only what our forefathers went through, but just this little bit of history should give you an idea of what this country will return to if you give up your Constitutional rights and let this Country return to a dictatorship. "Can't happen," you say? Wrong! It is happening right now. Every time you do not take the time to send an email or make a phone call to your Congressman to tell him to vote no on an important issue, you are part of the problem in this Country. Every time you do not take the time to go to the polls to vote, you are part of the problem in this Country. Every time you say "I don't have time," you are part of the problem in this Country. It takes everybody to fight back. Not just a few.

I do not know who wrote the following, but it is a good description of what an American is: 'An American is English, or French, or Italian, Irish, German, Spanish, Polish, Russian or Greek. An American may also be Canadian, Mexican, African, Indian, Chinese, Japanese, Korean, Australian, Iranian, Asian, or Arab, or Pakistani or Afghan.

An American may also be a Comanche, Cherokee, Osage, Blackfoot, Navaho, Apache, Seminole or one of the many other tribes known as Native Americans.

An American is Christian, or he could be Jewish, or Buddhist, or Muslim. In fact, there are more Muslims in America than in Afghanistan. The only difference is that in America they are free to worship as each of them chooses.

An American is also free to believe in no religion. For that he will answer only to God, not to the government, or to armed thugs claiming to speak for the government and for God.

An American lives in the most prosperous land in the history of the world. The root of that prosperity can be found in the Declaration of Independence, which recognizes the God given right of each person to the pursuit of happiness.

An American is generous. Americans have helped out just about every other nation in the world in their time of need, never asking a thing in return.

When Afghanistan was over-run by the Soviet army 20 years ago, Americans came with arms and supplies to enable the people to win back their country!

As of the morning of September 11, Americans had given more than any other nation to the poor in Afghanistan.

The national symbol of America, The Statue of Liberty, welcomes your tired and your poor, the wretched refuse of your teeming shores, the homeless, tempest tossed. These in fact are the people who built America.'

The Declaration of Independence

In Congress, July 4, 1776,
The unanimous Declaration of

The thirteen united States of America

When in the Course of human events, it becomes necessary for one people to dissolve the political bands which have connected them with another, and to assume among the powers of the earth, the separate an equal station to which the Laws of Nature and of Nature's God entitle them, a decent respect to the opinions of mankind requires that they should declare the causes which impel them to the separation.

We hold these truths to be self-evident, that all men are created equal, that they are endowed by their Creator with certain unalienable Rights, that among these are Life, Liberty and the pursuit of Happiness – That to secure these rights, Governments are instituted among Men, deriving their just powers from the consent of the governed, — That whenever any Form of Government becomes destructive of these ends, it is the Right of the People to alter or to abolish it, and to institute new Government, laying its foundation on such principles and organizing its powers in such form, as to them shall seem most likely to effect their Safety and Happiness, Prudence, indeed, will dictate that Governments long established should not be changed for light and transient causes; and accordingly all experience hast shewn, that mankind are more disposed to suffer, while evils are sufferable, than to right themselves by abolishing the forms to which they are accustomed. But when a long train of abuses and usurpations, pursuing invariably the same. Object evinces a design to reduce them under absolute Despotism, it is their right, it is their duty, to throw off such Government, and to provide new Guards for their future security. – Such has been the patient sufferance of these Colonies and such is now the necessity which constrains them to alter their former Systems of Government. The history of the present King of Great Britain is a history of repeated injuries and usurpations, all having in direct object the establishment of an absolute Tyranny over these States. To prove this, let Facts be submitted to a candid world.

He has refused his Assent to Laws, the most wholesome and necessary for the public good.

He has forbidden his Governors to pass Laws of immediate and pressing importance, unless suspended in their operation till his Assent should be obtained; and when so suspended, he has utterly neglected to attend to them.

He has refused to pass other Laws for the accommodation of large districts of people, unless those people would relinquish the right of Representation in the Legislature, a right inestimable to them and formidable to tyrants only.

He has called together legislative bodies at places unusual, uncomfortable, and distant from the depository of the public Records, for the sole purpose of fatiguing them into compliance with this measures.

He has dissolved Representative Houses repeatedly, for opposing with manly firmness his invasions on the rights of the people.

He has refused for a long time, after such dissolutions, to cause others to be elected; whereby the Legislative powers, incapable of Annihilation, have returned to the People at large for their exercise;

the State remaining in the mean time exposed to all the dangers of invasion from without, and convulsions within.

He has endeavoured to prevent the population of these States; for that purpose obstructing the Laws for Naturalization of Foreigners; refusing to pass others to encourage their migrations hither, and raising the conditions of new Appropriations of Lands.

He has obstructed the Administration of Justice, by refusing his Assent to Laws for establishing Judiciary powers.

He has made Judges dependent on his Will alone, for the tenure of their offices, and the amount and payment of their salaries.

He has erected a multitude of New Offices, and sent hither swarms of Officers to harass our people, and eat out their substance.

He has kept among us, in times of peace, Standing Armies without the Consent of our legislatures.

He has affected to render the Military independent of and superior to the Civil power.

He has combined with others to subject us to jurisdiction foreign to our constitution and unacknowledged by our laws; giving his Assent to their Acts of pretended Legislation:

For Quartering large bodies of armed troops among us:

For protecting them, by a mock Trial, from punishment for any Murders which they should commit on the Inhabitants of these States:

For cutting off our Trade with all parts of the world:

For imposing Taxes on us without our Consent:

For depriving us in many cases, of the benefits of Trial by Jury;

For transporting us beyond Seas to be tried for pretended offences:

For abolishing the free System of English Laws in a neighbouring Providence, establishing therein an Arbitrary government, and enlarging its Boundaries so as to render it at once an example and fit instrument for introducing the same absolute rule into these Colonies:

For taking away our Charters, abolishing our most valuable Laws, and altering fundamentally the Forms of our Governments:

For suspending our own Legislatures, and declaring themselves invested with power to legislate for us in all cases whatsoever.

He has abdicated Government here, by declaring us out of his Protection and waging War against us.

He has plundered our seas, ravaged our Coasts, burnt our towns, and destroyed the lives of our people.

He is at this time transporting large Armies of foreign Mercenaries to compleat the works of death, desolation and tyranny, already begun with circumstances of Cruelty & perfidy scarcely paralleled in the most barbarous ages, and totally unworthy the Head of a civilized nation.

He has constrained our fellow Citizens taken Captive on the high seas to bear arms against their Country, to become the executioners of their friends and Brethren, or to fall themselves by their Hands.

He has excited domestic insurrections amongst us, and has endeavoured to bring on the inhabitants of our frontiers, the merciless Indian Savages, whose known rule of warfare, is in undistinguished destruction of all ages, sexes and conditions.

In every stage of these Oppressions We have Petitioned for Redress in the most humble terms: Our repeated Petitions have been answered only by repeated injury. A Prince whose character is thus marked by every act which may define a Tyrant, is unfit to be the ruler of a free people.

Nor have We been wanting in attention to our Brittish brethren. We have warned them from time to time of attempts by their legislature to extend an unwarrantable jurisdiction over us. We have reminded them of the circumstances of our emigration and settlement here. We have appealed to their native justice and magnanimity and we have conjured them by the ties of our common kindred to disavow these usurpations, which, would inevitably interrupt our connections and correspondence. They too have been deaf to the voice of justice and of consanguinity. We must, therefore, acquiesce in the necessity, which denounces our Separation, and hold them,, as we hold the rest of mankind, Enemies in War, in Peace Friends.

We, therefore, the Representatives of the united States of America, in General Congress, Assembled, appealing to the Supreme Judge of the world for the rectitude of our intentions, do, in the Name, and by Authority of the good People of these Colonies, solemnly publish and declare, That these United Colonies are, and of Right out to be Free and Independent States; that they are Absolved from all Allegiance to the British Crown, and that all political connection between them and the State of Great Britain, is and out to be totally dissolved; and that as Free and Independent States, they have full Power to levy War, conclude Peace, contract Alliances, establish Commerce, and to do all other Acts and Things which Independent States may of right do. And for the support of this Declaration with a firm reliance on the protection of divine Providence, we mutually pledge to each other our Lives, our Fortunes and our Sacred Honor.

Connecticut	Samuel Huntington
	Roger Sherman
	William Williams
	Oliver Wolcott
Delaware	Thomas Mckean
	George Read
	Caesar Rodney
Georgia	Button Gwinnett
	Lyman Hall
	George Walton
Maryland	Charles Carroll of Carrollton
	Samuel Chase
	William Paca
	Thomas Stone
Massachusetts	John Adams
	Samuel Adams
	Elbridge Gerry John
	Hancock Robert
	Treat Paine

New Hampshire	Josiah Bartlett
	Matthew Thornton
	William Whipple
New Jersey	Abraham Clark
	John Hart
	Francis Hopkinson
	Richard Stockton
	John Witherspoon
New York	William Floyd
	Francis Lewis
	Philip Livingston
	Lewis Morris
North Carolina	Joseph Hewes
	William Hooper
	John Penn
Pennsylvania	George Clymer
	Benjamin Franklin
	Robert Morris
	John Morton
	George Ross
	Benjamin Rush
	James Smith
	George Taylor
	James Wilson
Rhode Island	William Ellery
	Stephen Hopkins
South Carolina	Thomas Heyward, Jr.
	Thomas Lynch, Jr.
	Arthur Middleton
	Edward Rutledge

Virginia	Carter Braxton
	Benjamin Harrison
	Thomas Jefferson
	Francis Lightfoot Lee
	Richard Henry Lee
	Thomas Nelson, Jr.
	George Wythe

The Constitution Of The United States

WE THE PEOPLE of the United States, in Order to form a more perfect Union, establish Justice, insure domestic Tranquility, provide for the common defence, promote the general Welfare, and secure the Blessings of Liberty to ourselves and our Posterity do ordain and establish this Constitution for the United State of America.

Article I

Section 1. All legislative Powers herein granted shall be vested in a Congress of the United States, which shall consist of a Senate and House of Representatives.

Section 2. The House of Representatives shall be composed of Members chosen every second Year by the People of the several States, and the Electors in each State shall have the Qualifications requisite for Electors of the most numerous Branch of the State Legislature.

No Person shall be a Representative who shall not have attained to the Age or twenty five Years and have seven Years a Citizen of the United States, and who shall not, when elected, be an Inhabitant of that State in which he shall be chosen.

[Representatives and direct Taxes shall be apportioned among the several States which may be included within this Union, according to their respective Numbers, which shall be determined by adding to the whole Numbers of free Persons, including those bound to Service for a Term of Years, and excluding Indians not taxed, three fifths of all other Persons.] The actual Enumeration shall be made within three Years after the first meeting of the Congress of the United States, and within every subsequent Term of ten Years, in such Manner as they shall by Law direct. The Number of Representatives shall not exceed one for every thirty Thousand, but each State shall have at Least one Representative, and until such enumeration shall be made, the State of New Hampshire shall be entitled to chuse three, Massachusetts eight, Rhode Island and Providence Plantations one, Connecticut five, New York six, New Jersey four, Pennsylvania eight, Delaware one, Maryland six, Virginia ten, North Carolina five, South Carolina five, and Georgia three.

When vacancies happen in the Representation of any State, the Executive Authority thereof shall issue Writs of Election to fill such Vacancies.

The House of Representatives shall chuse their Speaker and other Officers; and shall have the sole Power of Impeachment.

Section 3. The Senate of the United States shall be composed of two Senators from each State [chosen by the Legislature] thereof for six Years; and each Senator shall have one Vote.

Immediately after they shall be assembled in Consequence of the first Election, they shall be divided as equally as may be into three Classes. The Seats of the Senators of the First Class shall be vacated at the Expiration of the second Year, of the Second Class at the Expiration of the fourth Year, and of the third Class at the Expiration of the sixth Year, so that one third maybe chosen every second year; [and if Vacancies happen by Resignation, or otherwise, during the Recess of the Legislature of any State, the Executive thereof may make temporary Appointments until the next Meeting of the Legislature which shall then fill such Vacancies].

No person shall be a Senator who shall not have attained the age of thirty Years, and been nine years a Citizen of the United States, and who shall not when elected, be an inhabitant of that State for which he shall be chosen.

The Vice President of the United States shall be President of the Senate, but shall have no Vote, unless they be equally divided. The Senate shall chuse their other Officers and also a President pro tempore, in the Absence of the Vice President, or when he ***shall exercise the Office of President of the United States.***

The Senate shall have the sole Power to try all Impeachments. When sitting for that Purpose they shall be on Oath or Affirmation. When the President of the United States is tried, the Chief Justice shall preside: And no Person shall be convicted without the Concurrence of two thirds of the Members present Judgment in Cases of Impeachment shall not extend further than to removal from Office and disqualification to hold and enjoy any Office of honor, Trust or Profit under the United States: but the Party convicted shall nevertheless be liable and subject to Indictment, Trial, Judgment and Punishment according to Law.

Section 4. The Times, Places and Manner of holding Elections for Senators and Representatives, shall be prescribed in each State by the Legislature thereof; but the Congress may at any time by Law make or alter such Regulations, except as to the Places of chusing Senators.

Section 5. Each House shall be the Judge of the Elections. Returns and Qualifications of its own Members, and a Majority of each shall constitute a Quorum to do Business; but a smaller Number may adjourn from day to day, and may be authorized to compel the Attendance of absent Members, in such Manner, and under such Penalties as each House may provide.

Each House may determine the Rules as its Proceedings, punish its Members for disorderly Behaviour, and, with the Concurrence of two thirds, expel a Member.

Each House shall keep a Journal of its Proceedings, and from time to time publish the same, excepting such Parts as may in their Judgment require Secrecy; and the Yeas and Nays of the Members of either House on any question shall, at the Desire of one fifth of those Present, be entered on the Journal.

Neither House, during the Session of Congress shall, without the Consent of the other, adjourn for more than three days, nor to any other Place than that in which the two Houses shall be sitting.

Section 6. The Senators and Representatives shall receive a Compensation for their Services, to be ascertained by Law, and paid out of the Treasury of the United States. They shall in all Cases, except Treason, Felony and Breach of the Peace, be privileged from Arrest during their Attendance at the Session of their respective Houses, and in going to and returning from the same; and for any Speech or Debate in either House, they shall not be questioned in any other place.

No Senator or Representative shall, during the Time for which he was elected, be appointed to any civil Office under the Authority of the United States, which shall have been created, or the Emoluments whereof shall have been increased during such time; and no Person holding any Office under the United States shall be a Member of either house during his Continuance in Office.

Section 7. All Bills for raising Revenue shall originate in the House of Representatives; but the Senate may propose or concur with Amendments as on other Bills.

Every Bill which shall have passed the House of Representatives and the Senate, shall, before it becomes a Law, be presented to the President of the United States. If he approves he shall sign it, but if not he shall return it, with his Objections to that House in which it shall have originated, who shall enter the Objections at large on their Journal, and proceed to reconsider it. If after such Reconsideration two thirds of that House shall agree to pass the Bill, it shall be sent, together with the Objections, to the other House, by which it shall likewise be reconsidered, and if approved by two thirds of that House, it shall become a Law. But in all such Cases the Votes of both Houses shall be determined by yeas and Nays, and the Names of the Persons voting for and against the Bill shall be entered on the Journal of each

House respectively. If any Bill shall not be returned by the President within ten Days (Sunday excepted) after it shall have been presented to him, the Same shall be a Law, in like Manner as if he had signed it, unless the Congress by their Adjournment prevent its Return, in which Case it shall not be a Law.

Every Order, Resolution, or Vote to which the Concurrence of the Senate and House of Representatives may be necessary (except on a question of Adjournment) shall be presented to the President of the United States; and before the same shall take Effect, shall be approved by him, or being disapproved by him, shall be repassed by two thirds of the Senate and House of Representatives according to the Rules and limitations prescribed in the Case of a Bill.

Section 8. The Congress shall have Power to lay and Collect Taxes, Duties, Imposts and Excises, to pay the Debts and provide for the common Defence and general Welfare of the United States, but all Duties, Imposts and Excises shall be uniform throughout the United States;

To borrow Money on the credit of the United States;

To regulate Commerce with foreign Nations, and among the several States, and with the Indian Tribes;

To establish an uniform Rule of Naturalization and uniform Laws on the subject of Bankruptcies throughout the United States;

To coin Money, regulate the Value thereof, and of foreign Coin, and fix the Standard of Weights and Measures;

To provide for the Punishment of counterfeiting the Securities and current coin of the United States;

To establish the Post Office and post Roads;

To promote the Progress of Science and useful Arts,by securing for limited Times to Authors and Inventors the exclusive Right to their respective Writings and Discoveries;

To constitute Tribunals inferior to the supreme Court;

To define and punish Piracies and Felonies committed on the high seas and Offences against the Law of Nations;

To declare War, grant Letters of Marque and Reprisal, and make Rules concerning Captures on Land and Water;

To raise and support Armies, but no Appropriation of Money to that Use shall be for a longer Term than two Years;

To provide and maintain a Navy;

To make Rules for the Government and Regulation of the land and naval Forces;

To provide for organizing, arming and disciplining, the militia, and for governing such Part of them as may be employed in the Service of the United States, reserving to the States respectively, the Appointment of the Officers, and the Authority of training the Militia according to the discipline prescribed by Congress;

To exercise exclusive Legislation in all Cases whatsoever, over such District (not exceeding ten Miles square) as may, by Cession of particular States, and the Acceptance of Congress, become the Seat of the Government of the United States, and to exercise like Authority over all Places purchased by the Consent of the Legislature of the State in which the Same shall be, for the Erection of Forts, Magazines, Arsenals, dock-Yards, and other needful Buildings – And

To make all Laws which shall be necessary and proper for carrying into Execution the foregoing Powers and all other Powers vested by this Constitution in the Government of the United States, or in any Department or Officer thereof.

Section 9. The Migration or Importation of such Persons as any of the States now existing shall think proper to admit, shall not be prohibited by the Congress prior to the Year one thousand eight hundred and eight, but Tax or duty may be imposed on such Importation, not exceeding ten dollars for each Person.

The Privilege of the Writ of Habeas Corpus shall not be suspended, unless when in Cases of Rebellion or Invasion the public Safety may require it.

No Bill of Attainder or ex post facto Law shall be passed. No Capitation, or other direct, Tax shall be paid [unless in Proportion to the Census or enumeration herein before directed to be taken].

No Tax or Duty shall be laid on Articles exported from any State.

No Preferences shall be given by any Regulation of Commerce or Revenue to the Ports of one State over those of another; nor shall Vessels bound to, or from one State, be obliged to enter, clear, or pay Duties in another.

No Money shall be drawn from the Treasury, but in Consequence of Appropriations made by Law; and a regular Statement and Account of the Receipts and Expenditures of all public Money shall be published from time to time.

No Title of Nobility shall be granted by the United States: And no Person holding any Office of Profit or Trust under them, shall, without the Consent of the Congress, accept of any present, Emolument, Officer, or Title, of any kind whatever, from any King, Prince, or foreign State.

Virginia	John Blair
	James Madison Jr.
North Carolina	Wm. Blount
	Richd. Dobbs Spaight
	Hu Williamson
South Carolina	J. Rutledge
	Charles Cotesworth Pinckney
	Charles Pinckney

Section 10. No State shall enter into any Treaty, Alliance, or Confederation; grant Letters of Marque and Reprisal; coin money; emit Bills of Credit; make any Thing but gold and silver Coin a Tender in Payment of Debts; pass any Bill of Attainder, ex post facto Law, or Law impairing the Obligation of Contracts, or grant any Title of Nobility.

No State shall, without the Consent of the Congress, lay any Imposts or Duties on Imports or Exports, except what may be absolutely necessary for executing its inspection Laws and the net Produce of all Duties and Imposts, laid by any State on Imports or Exports, shall be for the Use of the Treasury of the United States; and all such Laws shall be subject to the Revision and Control of the Congress.

No State shall, without the Consent of Congress, lay any Duty of Tonnage, keep Troops, or Ships of War in Time of Peace, enter into any Agreement or Compact with another State, or with a foreign Power, or engage in War, unless actually invaded, or in such imminent Danger as will not admit of delay.

Article II

Section 1. The executive Power shall be vested in a President of the United States of America. He shall hold his Office during the term of four Years, and, together with the Vice President, chosen for the same Term, be elected as follows:

Each State shall appoint, in such Manner, as the Legislature thereof may direct, a Number of Electors, equal to the whole Number of Senators and Representatives to which the State may be entitled in the Congress: but no Senator or Representative, or Person holding an Office of Trust or Profit under the United States shall be appointed an Elector.

The Electors shall meet in their respective States, and vote by Ballot for two Persons, of whom one at least shall not be an Inhabitant of the same State with themselves. And they shall make a List of all the Persons voted for, and of the Number of Votes for each; which List they shall sign and certify and transmit sealed to the Seat of the Government of the United States, directed to the President of the Senate. The President of the Senate shall, in the Presence of the Senate and House of Representatives, open all the Certificates, and the Votes shall then be counted. The Person having the greatest Number of Votes shall be the President. If such Number be a Majority of the whole Number of Electors appointed; and there be no more than one who have such Majority; and have an equal Number of Votes, then the House of Representatives shall immediately chuse by Ballot one of them for President; and if no Person have a Majority, then from the five highest on the List the said House shall in like Manner chuse the President. But in chusing the President, the Votes shall be taken by State, the Representation from each State having one Vote; A quorum for this purpose all consist of a Member or Members from two thirds of the State, and a Majority of all the States shall be necessary to a Choice. In every Case, after the Choice of the President, the Person having the greatest Number of Votes of the Electors shall be the Vice President. But if there should remain two or more who have equal votes, the Senate shall chuse from them by Ballot the Vice President.

The Congress may determine the Time of chusing the Electors, and the Day on which they shall give their Votes; which Day shall be the same throughout the United States.

No person except a natural born Citizen, or a Citizen of the United States, at the time of the Adoption of this Constitution shall be eligible to the Office of President; neither shall any Person be eligible to that Office who shall not have attained to the Age of thirty five Years, and been fourteen Years a Resident within the United States.

[In Case of the Removal of the President from Office, or of his Death, Resignation, or Inability to discharge the Powers and Duties of the said Office, the Same shall devolve on the Vice President, and the Congress may by Law provide for the Case of Removal, Death, Resignation or Inability, both of the President and Vice President, declaring what Officer shall then act as President, and such Officer shall act accordingly, until the Disability be removed, or a President shall be elected.]

The President shall, at stated Times, receive for his Services, a Compensation, which shall neither be increased nor diminished during the Period for which he shall have been elected, and he shall not receive within that Period any other Emolument from the United States or any of them.

Before he enter on the Execution of his Office, he shall take the following Oath or Affirmation: — "I do solemnly swear (or affirm) that I will faithfully execute the Office of President of the United States and will to the best of my Ability preserve, protect and defend the Constitution of the United States."

Section 2. The President shall be Commander in Chief of the Army
and Navy of the United States, and of the Militia of the several
States, when called into the actual Service of the United States;
he may require the Opinion, in writing, of the principal Officer
in each of the executive Departments, upon any subject relat-
ing to the Duties of their respective Offices, and he shall have
Power to grant Reprieves and Pardons for Offences against the
United States, except in Cases of Impeachment.

He shall have power, by and with the Advice and Consent of the
Senate, to make Treaties, provided two thirds of the Senators pres-
ent concur; and he shall nominate, and by and with the Advice and
Consent of the Senate shall appoint Ambassadors and other public
Ministers and Consuls, Judges of the supreme Court, and all other
Officers of the United States, whose Appointments are not herein
otherwise provided for, and which shall be established by law; but
the Congress may by Law vest the Appointment of such inferior
Officers, as they think proper in the President alone, in the Courts of
Law, or in the Heads of Departments.

The President shall have Power to fill up all Vacancies that may
happen during the Recess of the Senate, by granting Commissions
which shall expire at the end of their next Session. Section 3. He shall
from time to time give to the Congress Information of the State of
the Union, and recommend to their Consideration such Measures
as he shall judge necessary and expedient; he may, on extraordinary Occasions, convene both Houses, or either of them, and in
Case of Disagreement between them, with Respect to the Time of
Adjournment, he may adjourn them to such Time as he shall think
proper; he shall receive Ambassadors and other public Ministers;
he shall take Care that the Laws be faithfully executed, and shall
Commission all the Officers of the United States. Section 4. The
President, Vice President, and all civil Officers of the United States,
shall be removed from Office on Impeachment for, and Conviction
of Treason, Bribery, or other high Crimes and Misdemeanors.

Article III

Section 1. The judicial Power of the United States shall be vested in one supreme Court, and in such inferior Courts as the Congress may from time to time ordain and establish. The Judges, both of the supreme and inferior Courts, shall hold their Offices during good behavior, and shall, at stated Times, receive for their Services a Compensation, which shall not be diminished during their Continuance in Office.

Section 2. The judicial Power shall extend to all Cases, in Law and Equity, arising under this Constitution, the Law of the United States, and Treaties made, or which shall be made, under their Authority; — to all Cases affecting Ambassadors, other public Ministers and Consuls; — to Controversies to which the United States shall be a party;–to Controversies between two or more States; —[between a State and Citizens of another State;] – between Citizens of different States; — between Citizens of the same State claiming Lands under Grants of different States, [and between a State, or the Citizens thereof, and foreign States, Citizens or Subjects.]

In all Cases affecting Ambassadors, other pubic Ministers, other public Ministers and Consuls, and those in which a State shall be Party, the supreme Court shall have original jurisdiction. In all the other Cases before mentioned, the supreme Court shall have appellate Jurisdiction, both as to Law and Fact, with such Exceptions, and under such Regulation Laws the Congress shall make.

The Trial of all Crimes, except in Cases of Impeachment, shall be by Jury; and such Trial shall be held in the State where the said Crime shall have been committed; but when not committed within any State, the Trial shall be at such Place or Places as the Congress may by Law have directed.

Section 3. Treason against the United States, shall consist only in levying War against them, or in adhering to their Enemies, giving them Aid and Comfort. No Person shall be convicted of

Treason unless on the Testimony of two Witnesses to the same overt Act, or on Confession in Open Court. The Congress shall have Power to declare the Punishment of Treason, but no Attainder of Treason shall work Corruption of Blood, or Forfeiture except during the Life of the Person attainted.

Article IV

Section 1. Full Faith and Credit shall be given in each State to the public Acts, Records and judicial Proceedings of every other State. And Congress may by general Laws prescribe the Manner in which such Acts, Records and Proceedings shall be proved, and the Effect thereof.

Section 2. The Citizens of each State shall be entitled to all Privileges and immunities of Citizens in the several States.

A person charged in any State with Treason, Felony, or other Crime, who shall flee from Justice and be found in another State, shall on Demand of the executive Authority of the State from which he fled, be delivered up, to be removed to the State having Jurisdiction of the Crime.

[No Person held to the Service or Labour in one State, under the Laws thereof, escaping into another, shall, in consequence of any Law or regulation therein, be discharged from such Service or Labour, but shall be delivered up on Claim of the Party to whom such Service or Labour may be due.]

Section 3. New States may be admitted by the Congress into this Union; but no new State shall be formed or erected within the Jurisdiction of any other State, nor any State be formed by the Junction of two or more States, or Parts of States, without the Consent of the Legislature of the States concerned as well as of the Congress.

The Congress shall have Power to dispose of and make all needful Rules and Regulations respecting the Territory of other Property belonging to the United States; and nothing in this Constitution shall be construed as to Prejudice any Claims of the United States or any particular State.

Section 4. The United States shall guarantee to every State in this Union a Republican Form of Government, and shall protect each of them against invasion; and on Application of the Legislature, or of the Executive (when the Legislature cannot be convened) against domestic Violence.

Article V

The Congress, whenever two thirds of both Houses shall deem it necessary, shall propose Amendments to this Constitution, or on the Application of the Legislatures of two thirds of the several States, shall call a Convention for proposing Amendments, which in either Case, shall be valid in all Intents and Purposes, as Part of this Constitution, when ratified by the Legislature of three fourths of the several States, or by Conventions in three fourths thereof, as the one or the other Mode of Ratification may be proposed by the Congress; Provided that no Amendment which may be made prior to the Year One Thousand eight hundred and eight shall in any Manner affect the first and fourth Clauses in the Ninth Section of the first Article; and that no State, without its Consent, shall be deprived of its equal Suffrage in the Senate.

Article VI

All Debts contracted and Engagements entered into, before the Adoption of this Constitution, shall be as valid against the United States under this Constitution, as under the Confederation.

This Constitution, and the Laws of the United States which shall be made in Pursuance thereof; and all Treaties made, or which shall be made, under the Authority of the United Sates, shall be the supreme Law of the Land; and the Judges in every State shall be bound thereby, any Thing in the Constitution or Laws of any State to the contrary notwithstanding.

The Senators and Representatives before mentioned, and the Members of the several State Legislatures, and all executives and judicial Officers, both of the United States and several States, shall be bound by Oath or Affirmation, to support this Constitution; but no religious Test shall ever be required as a Qualification to any Officer or public Trust under the United States.

Article VII

The Ratification of the Conventions of nine States shall be sufficient for the Establishment of the Constitution between the States so ratifying the Same.

Done in Convention by the Unanimous Consent of the State present the Seventeenth Day of September in the Year of our Lord one thousand seven hundred eighty seven and of the Independence of the United States of America the Twelfth In witness whereof We have hereunto subscribed our Names.

G. Washington
President and deputy from Virginia

Delaware	George Read
	Gunning Bedford
	Jun John
	Dickinson Richard
	Bassett Jaco: Broom

Amendment XII

The Electors shall meet in their respective states and vote by ballot for President and Vice President, one of whom, at least, shall not be an inhabitant of the same state with themselves; they shall name in their ballots the person voted for as President and in distinct ballots the person voted for as Vice President, and they shall make distinct lists of all persons voted for as President, and of all persons voted for as Vice President, and of the number of votes for each, which lists they shall sign and certify, and transmit sealed to the seat of the government of the United States, directed to the President of the Senate; — the President of the Senate shall, in the presence of the Senate and the House of Representatives, open all the certificate and the votes shall then be counted; — the person having the greatest number of votes for President, shall be the President, if such number be a majority of the whole number of Electors appointed; and if no person have such majority, then from the persons having the highest numbers not exceeding three on the list of those voted for as President, the house of Representatives shall choose immediately, by ballot the President. But in choosing the president, the votes shall be taken by states, the representation from each state having one vote; a quorum for this purpose shall consist of a member or members from two-thirds of the states, and a majority of all the states shall be necessary to choose. [And if the House of Representatives shall not choose a President whenever the right of choice shall devolve upon them before the fourth day of March next following, then the Vice President shall act as President, as in case of the death or other constitutional disability of the President,. —] The person having the greatest number of votes as Vice President, if such number be a majority of the whole number of Electors appointed, and if no person have a majority, then from the two highest numbers on the list, the Senate shall choose the Vice President; a quorum for the purpose shall consist of two-thirds of the whole number of Senators, and a majority of the whole number shall be necessary to a choice. But no person constitutionally ineligible to the office of President shall be eligible to that of Vice President of the United States.

Maryland	James McHenry
	Dan of St Thos.
	Jenifer Danl Carroll
	Pierce Butler
Georgia	William Few
	Abr Baldwin

New Hampshire	John Langdon
	Nicholas Gilman
Massachusettes	Nathaniel Gorham
	Rufus King
Connecticut	Wm. Saml. Johnson
	Roger Sherman
New York	Alexander Hamilton
New Jersey	Wil: Livingston
	David Brearley
	Wm. Paterson
	Jona: Dayton
Pennsylvania	B Franklin
	Thomas Mifflin
	Robt Morris Geo.
	Clymer Thos.
	FitzSimons Jared
	Ingersoll James
	Wilson Gouv
	Morris
	Attest William Jackson Secretary

Amendments To The
Constitutions Of
The United States

Amendment I

Congress shall make no law respecting an establishment of religion, or prohibiting the free exercise thereof; or abridging the freedom of speech, or of the press, or the right of the people peaceably to assemble, and to petition the Government for a redress of grievances.

Amendment II

A well regulated Militia, being necessary to the security of a free State, the right of the people to keep and bear Arms, shall not be infringed.

Amendment III

No Soldier shall, in time of peace, be quartered in any house, without the consent of the Owner, nor in time of war, but in a manner to be prescribed by law.

Amendment IV

The right of the people to be secure in their persons houses papers, and effects, against unreasonable searches and seizures, shall not be violated, and no Warrants shall issue, but upon probable cause, supported by Oath or affirmation, and particularly describing the place to be searched, and the persons or things to be seized.

Amendment V

No person shall be held to answer for a capital, or otherwise infamous crime, unless on a presentment or indictment of a Grand Jury, except in cases arising in the land or naval forces, or in the Militia, when in actual service in time of War or public danger; nor shall any person be subject for the same offence to be twice put in jeopardy of life or limb; nor shall be compelled in any criminal case to be a witness against himself,nor be deprived of life, liberty, or property, without due process of law; nor shall private property be taken for public use, without just compensation.

Amendment VI

In all criminal prosecutions, the accused shall enjoy the right to a speedy and public trial,by an impartial jury of the State and district wherein the crime shall have been committed which district shall have been previously ascertained by law, and to be informed of the nature and cause of the accusation; to be confronted with the witnesses against him; to have compulsory process for obtaining witnesses in his favor and to have the Assistance of Counsel for his defence.

Amendment VII

In Suits at Common law, where the value in controversy shall exceed twenty dollars, the right of trial by jury shall be preserved, and no fact tried by a jury, shall be otherwise re-examined in any Court of the United States, than according to the rules of the common law.

Amendment VIII

Excessive bail shall not be required, nor excessive fines imposed, nor cruel and unusual punishments inflicted.

Amendment IX

The enumeration in the Constitution, of certain rights, shall not be construed to deny or disparage others retained by the people.

Amendment X

The powers not delegated to the United States by the Constitution, nor prohibited by it to the States, are reserved to the States respectively, or to the people.

Amendment XI

The Judicial power of the United States shall not be construed to extend to any suit in law or equity commenced or prosecuted against one of the United States by Citizens of another State, or by Citizens or Subjects of any Foreign State.

Amendment XIII

Section I. Neither slavery nor involuntary servitude, except as a punishment for crime whereof the party shall have been duly convicted, shall exist within the United States, or any place subject to their jurisdiction.

Section 2. Congress shall have power to enforce this article by appropriate legislation.

Amendment XIV

Section 1. All persons born or naturalized in the United States, and subject to the jurisdiction thereof, are citizens of the United States and of the State wherein they reside. No State shall make or enforce any law which shall abridge the privilege or immunities of citizens of the United States; nor shall any State deprive any person of life, liberty, or property, without due process of law; nor deny to any person within its jurisdiction the equal protection of the laws.

Section 2. Representatives shall be apportioned among the several States according to their respective numbers, counting the whole number of persons in each State, excluding Indians not taxed. But when the right to vote at any election for the choice of electors for President and vice President of the United States, Representatives in Congress, the Executive and Judicial Officers of a State, or the Members of the Legislature thereof, is denied to any of the male inhabitants of such State, being twenty-one years of age, and citizens of the United States or in any way abridged, except for participation in rebellion, or other crime, the basis of representation therein shall be reduced in the proportion which the number of such male citizens shall bear to the whole number of male citizens twenty-one years of age in such State.

Section 3. No person shall be a Senator or Representative in Congress or elector of President and Vice President, or hold any office civil or military, under the United States, or under any State, who have previously taken an oath, as a member of Congress, or as an officer of the United States, or as a member of any State legislature, or as an executive or judicial officer of any State, to support the Constitution of the united States, shall have engaged in insurrection or rebellion against the same, or given aid or comfort to the enemies thereof. But Congress may by a vote of two-thirds of each House, remove such disability.

Section 4. The validity of the public debt of the United States, authorized by law, including debts incurred for payment of pensions and bounties for services in suppressing insurrection or rebellion, shall not be questioned. But neither the United States not any State shall assume or pay any debt or obligation incurred in aid of insurrection or rebellion against the United States, or any claim for the loss or emancipation of any slave; but all such debts, obligations and claims shall be held illegal and void.

Section 5. The Congress shall have the power to enforce, by appropriate legislation, the provisions of this article.

Amendment XV

Section 1. The right of citizens of the United States to vote shall not be denied or abridged by the United States or by any State on account of race, color, or previous condition or servitude –

Section 2. The Congress shall have the power to enforce this article by appropriate legislation.

Article XVI

The Congress shall have the power to lay and collect taxes on incomes, from whatever source derived, without apportionment among the several States, and without regard to any census or enumeration.

Article XVII

The Senate of the United States shall be composed of two Senators from each State, elected by the people thereof, for six years, and each Senator shall have one vote. The electors in each State shall have the qualifications requisite for electors of the most numerous branches of the State legislatures.

When vacancies happen in the representation of any State in the Senate, the executive authority of such State shall issue writs of election to fill such vacancies: Provided, That the legislature of any State may empower the executive thereof to make temporary appointments until the people fill the vacancies by election as the legislature may direct.

This amendment shall not be so construed as to affect the election or term of any Senator chosen before it becomes valid as part of the Constitution.

Amendment XVIII

Section 1. After one year from the ratification of this article the manufacture, sale, or transportation of intoxicating liquors within, the importation thereof into, or the exportation thereof from the United States, and all t4erritory subject to the jurisdiction thereof for beverage purposes is hereby prohibited.

Section 2. The Congress and the several States shall have concurrent power to enforce this Article by appropriate legislation.

Section 3. This article shall be inoperative unless it shall have been ratified as an amendment to the Constitution by the legislature of the several States as provided in the Constitution within seven years from the date of the submission hereof to the States by the Congress.

Amendment XIX

The right of citizens of the United States to vote shall not be denied or abridged by the United States or any State on account of sex. Congress shall have power to enforce this article by appropriate legislation.

Amendment XX

Section 1. The terms of the President and the Vice President shall end at noon on the 20th day of January, and the terms of Senators and Representatives at noon on the 3rd day of January of the years in which such terms would have ended if this article had not been ratified and the terms of their successors shall then begin

Section 2. The Congress shall assemble at least once in every year and such meeting shall begin at noon on the 3rd day of January, unless they shall by law appoint a different day.

Section 3. If, at the time fixed for the beginning of the term of the President, the President elect shall have died, the Vice President elect shall become President. If a President shall not have been chosen before the time fixed for the beginning of his term, or if the President elect shall have failed to qualify, then the Vice President elect shall act as President until a President shall have qualified; and the Congress may by law provide for the case wherein neither a resident elect nor a Vice President shall have qualified, declaring who shall then act as President, or the manner in which one who is to act shall be selected, and such person shall act accordingly until a President or Vice President shall have qualified.

Section 4. The Congress may by law provide for the case of the death of any of the persons from whom the House of Representatives may choose a President whenever the right of choice shall have devolved upon them, and for the case of the death of any of the persons from whom the Senate may choose a Vice President whenever the right of choice shall have devolved upon them.

Section 5. Sections 1 and 2 shall take effect on the 15thy day of October following the ratification of this article.

Section 6. This article shall be inoperative unless it shall have been ratified as an amendment to the Constitution by the legislature of three-fourths of the several states within seven years from the date of its submission.

Amendment XXI

Section 1. The Eighteenth Article of Amendment to the Constitution if hereby repealed.

Section 2. The transportation of importation into any State, Territory, or Possession of the United States for delivery or use therein of intoxicating liquors, in violation of the laws thereof, is hereby prohibited.

Section 3.This article shall be inoperative unless it shall have been ratified as an amendment to the Constitution by convention in the several states as provided in the Constitution, within seven years from the dat4e of the submissio0n hereof to the States by the Congress. [The 21st Amendment was ratified December 5, 1933]

Amendment XXII

Section 1. No person shall be elected to the office of the President more than twice, and no person who has held the office of President, or acted as President, for more than two years of a term to which some other person was elected President shall be elected to the office of President more than once. But this Article shall not apply to any person holding the office of President when this Article was proposed by Congress, and shall not prevent any person who may be holding the office of President, or acting as President, during the term within which this Article becomes operative from holding the office of President or acting as President during the remainder of such term.

Section 2. This article shall be inoperative unless it shall have been ratified as an amendment to the Constitution by the legislature of three-fourths of the several States within seven years from the date of its submission to the States by the Congress.

Amendment XXIII

Section 1. The District constituting the seat of Government of the United States shall appoint in such manner as Congress may direct:

A number of electors of President and Vice President equal to the whole number of Senators and Representatives in Congress to which the District would be entitled if it were a State, but in no event more than the least populous State; they shall be in addition to those appointed by the States, but they shall be considered, for the purposes of the election of President and Vice President, to be electors appointed by a State; and they shall meet in the District and perform such duties as provided by the twelfth article of amendment.

Section 2. The Congress shall have power to enforce this article by appropriate legislation.

Amendment XXIV

Section 1. The right of citizens of the United States to vote in any primary or other election for President or Vice President, for electors for President or Vice President, or for Senator or Representative in Congress, shall not be denied or abridged by the United States or any State by reason or failure to pay poll tax or other tax.

Section 2. The Congress shall have power to enforce this article by appropriate legislation.

Amendment XXV

Section 1. In case of the removal of the President from office or of his death or resignation, the Vice President shall become President.

Second 2. Whenever there is a vacancy in the office of the Vice President, the President shall nominate a Vice President who shall take office upon confirmation by a majority of both Houses of Congress.

Section 3. Whenever the President transmits to the President pro tempore of the Senate and the Speaker of the House of Representatives his written declaration that he is unable to discharge the powers and duties of his office, and until he transmits to them a written declaration to the contrary, such powers and duties shall be discharged by the Vice President as Acting President.

Section 4. Whenever the Vice President and a majority of either the principal officers of the executive departments or of such other body as Congress may by law provide, transmit to the President pro tempore of the Senate and the Speaker of the House of Representatives their written declaration that the President is unable to discharge the powers and duties of his office, the Vice President shall immediately assume the powers and duties of the office as Acting President.

Thereafter, when the President transmits to the President pro tempore of the Senate and the Speaker of the House of Representatives his written declaration that no inability exists, he shall resume the powers and duties of his office unless the Vice President and a majority of either the principal officers of the executive department or of such other body as Congress may by law provide,transmit within four days to the President pro tempore of the Senate and the Speaker of the House of Representatives their written declaration that the President is unable to discharge the powers and duties of his office. Thereupon Congress shall decide the issue, assembling within forty-eight hours for that purpose if not in session. If the Congress, within twenty-one days after receipt of the latter written declaration, or, of Congress is not in session, within twenty-one days after Congress is required to assemble, determines by two-thirds vote of both Houses that the President is unable to discharge the powers and duties of his office, the Vice President shall continue to discharge the same as Acting President; otherwise, the President shall resume the powers and duties of his office.

Amendment XXVI

Section 1.The right of citizens of the United States,who are eighteen years of age or older, to vote shall not be denied or abridged by the United States or by any State on account of age.

Section 2. The Congress shall have power to enforce this Article by appropriate legislation.

Amendment XXVII

No law, varying the compensation for the services of the Senators and Representatives, shall take effect, until an election of representatives shall have intervened.

www.ingramcontent.com/pod-product-compliance
Lightning Source LLC
Chambersburg PA
CBHW062127020426
42335CB00013B/1129